SUPER HAIRO

NIKKI CESTARO

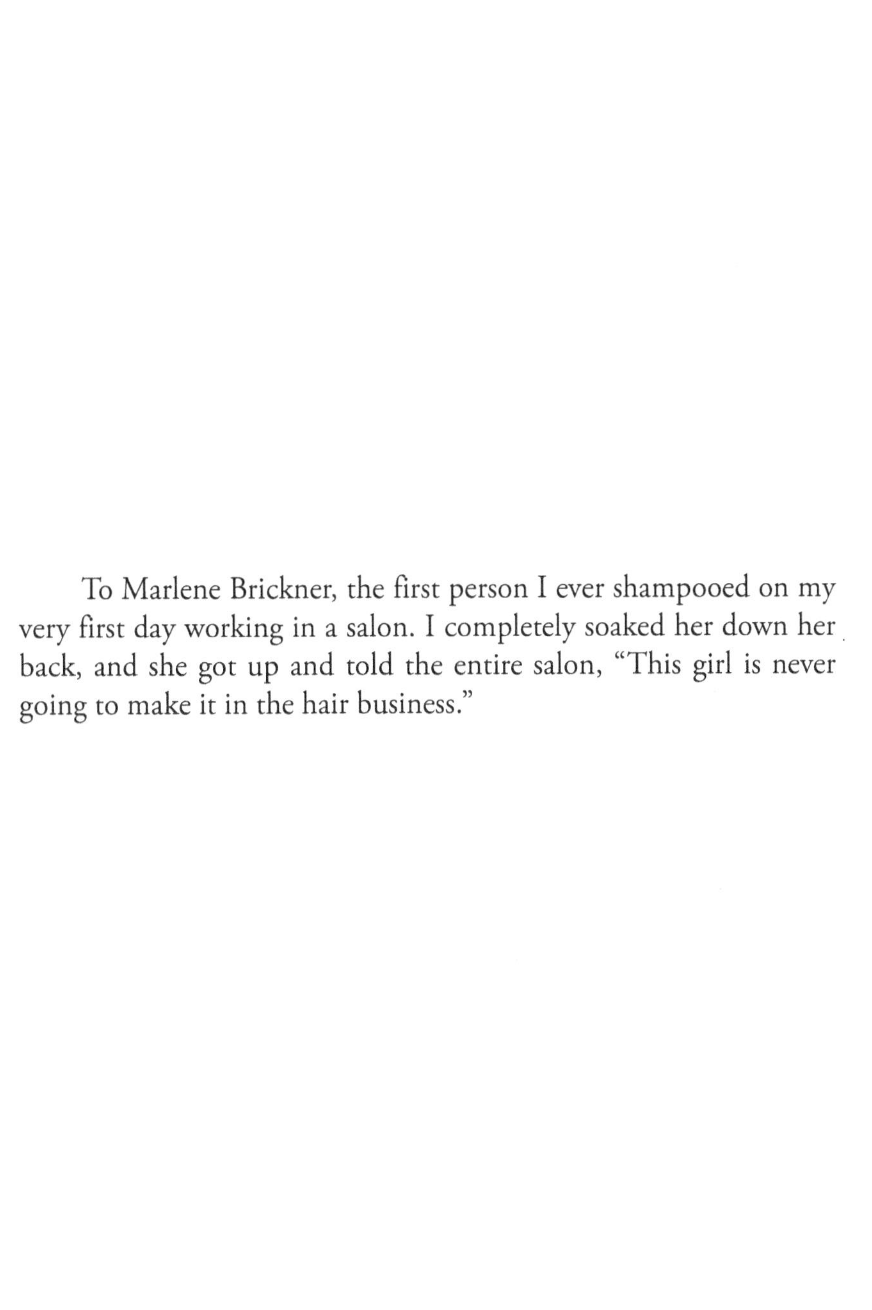

To Marlene Brickner, the first person I ever shampooed on my very first day working in a salon. I completely soaked her down her back, and she got up and told the entire salon, "This girl is never going to make it in the hair business."

Contents

At the end of the day, I am merely just a person. I get up every morning with the same goals as everybody else. Eat smart so I can finally lose those five pounds. Drink enough water. Try to work out three to four times a week to keep my body in tune for my job. Get to work on time so I could attempt to do my hair properly. Call my mother. Don't curse. Be nice and stay calm. Take at least ten minutes a day to close my eyes and quiet my mind, stop and smell the roses, blah, blah, blah.

Fast-forward to fourteen hours later, I'm exhausted, hair not done and still in the wet bun from this morning, and clothes are covered in hair and stained with hair color. A Wendy's drive-thru bag on my passenger seat, and I'm looking at the same water bottle in the cup holder, unfinished from this morning. Hey, at least I got to work on time. And those few minutes to close my eyes and meditate? I used them while I waited for my dinner feed bag on the drive-thru line.

It's a hairy life—the life I chose, the life that I created. I love my career, and owning a salon was my ultimate dream. I wake up each day excited to see my staff and my clients, and I'm always inspired to do work I love. But if I actually sit back and think of all I need/expect/have/want/am expected to accomplish and describe it as if it's someone else's life, I would actually feel bad for that person. I'd give them a hug and find them a great therapist.

As a hairdresser, I'm expected to create magic every thirty minutes behind the chair. It's my job to make a client feel better than they did when they walked in—execute a miracle to make them look like one of the inauthentic, filtered insta-pics that they will most certainly show me. I become a mad scientist, formulating and reformulating bowls of goop in a crowded back room, returning with a magic wand to create a customized hair-color masterpiece. I can only hope that my assistant showed up to work, so I have the appropriate help to get the job done. Maintaining a positive attitude and a sparkling personality while standing in heels, I work quickly to stay on time for the next pending client, all the while needing to pee for well over an hour. And absolutely not, under any circumstances, can I call in sick. You see, hairdressers are immortal. We are not allowed to be sick or cancel on a client last minute.

Now throw in the responsibilities of owning this business. Worrying about having enough product, about the splotches of color staining the floor, the towel laundry getting backed up, the shampoo sinks getting clogged, unsatisfied clients, running out of toilet paper in the bathroom, screwed-up appointments, wondering which of my employees or their kids will be home sick, the multiple boxes of deliveries arriving and needing to be unpacked, relying on which assistant will be able to work, the Wi-Fi going down, clients coming late, and having to micromanage every little detail throughout every single day…all while I'm doing hair on clients all day long behind the chair—it's enough to make me want to check into an insane asylum. Let's add in the business aspect of accounting, payroll, bookkeeping, supply ordering, liability, and insurance that I am responsible for. Just thinking about it all is giving me an anxiety attack. But who has time for that? My next client is due in five minutes.

But I chose this path. When I entered the hair business, I knew it wouldn't be easy. I've always had the personality to take charge and multitask, the stamina to withstand long days and curveballs that are thrown my way. I was a bossy child, and I think I was destined to lead. It's the responsible Capricorn in me to take on chaos and figure it all out. And I'm good at it. Granted, this industry isn't for everybody because the moment you become weak, it can swallow you up alive.

Transitioning from employee to employer was a lesson to be learned. It's quite different being just a busy hairdresser who works on clients every day to the boss of this tiny empire, still working behind the chair as usual but responsible for every detail that goes on all day every day. Every hair service that is done, whether by me or one of my stylists, becomes my responsibility if a client is not happy. Every bottle of shampoo we sell becomes my problem if the person is dissatisfied. If the light bulb blew by a station, it's my job to swiftly change it so we continue on as usual. Payday is coming. Who figures out all of the numbers and takes care of payroll? This girl right here!

All are necessary but constant and wildly consuming. In order to run a business smoothly, someone has to paddle their ass off to keep it going, so it's my ass that is in constant motion. Knowing that most times, he has to take second place when it comes to my work, my husband has always said, "You might not be the best at it, but there is nobody better." I like to think he is right. I've made many mistakes along the way, but I learned from each of them. No one said it was easy, but when it runs well, it's rewarding as hell. And when it doesn't, I keep the liquor stores in business.

I learned a lot the hard way. I am their boss, not their friend. It is my signature on their paycheck. To them, it's a job; to me, it's my life. They put their scissors down at the end of the day and go on with their lives. At the end of my day, I'm up all night doing paper-work, payroll, orders, social media posting, and accounting—while occasionally trying to numb my mind and catch up on *The Real Housewives* of whatever city that is current—as I finish what's left in the fast-food bag I picked up on my way home from work. It might sound maddening to be in constant motion all day, and I agree that sometimes, it all is. But in a crazy way, I am fueled by all the chaos. Either I'm clinically insane, or I've become used to it, because I don't think I would have it any other way.

I work hard so I can appreciate my downtime. It's a rarity to have extra time to enjoy, but when I do, I know exactly how to spend it. I'm a major foodie; I've been food obsessed my whole life. I love sitting in a restaurant, any restaurant at all. I'm turned on by a menu, looking forward to the people watching, fully intoxicated by the atmosphere. I find myself watching the staff as they work together in unison, like performing a dance. I have tremendous respect for the food industry as another entity of personalized service business.

There is no *I* in team, and as one professional service provider to another, I know it takes skill, sacrifice, and passion to make it all work. I enjoy experiencing the effort that is needed to execute every dish to arrive for each diner, knowing like as it is in a salon, it takes a village to get the job done.

I love an all-day food-and-drink crawl from NYC to the North Fork of Long Island. I can regularly pull off a marathon of dining in three to four restaurants in one day. I pride myself on knowing almost every restaurant on Long Island, and sometimes, I can even tell you what's best to order. Many clients treat me as if I'm their personal concierge, reaching out to me at random times, requesting recommendations to various places for all different occasions. I always keep my ears open for new and exciting restaurants to try. I'm always happy to support my favorite dining establishments and excited to share my experiences with my friends, so I recommend to all who ask.

My close friends have dubbed me "Julie, the cruise director," stemming from my love of planning. I love getting out and being sociable, a common luxury that I found I had to give up owning a business due to my lack of time. But as a born planner, I make good use of my limited time and plan fun events to enjoy with people I love to hang out with.

I try to work out a few times a week, fitting in Pilates to balance out my excessive love of eating. Coincidentally, it helps keep my body and posture in tune for the hours I need to spend behind the chair. Physical health is very important as a hairdresser and even more so when you dine out as much I do. Aside from working off all the food I am so passionate about, staying in shape builds great core strength, helping to support my body to move and function as I need to in this line of work and to help keep me standing all day long. And at my age, its toning benefits are nonnegotiable.

As much as I love being out and about, I am a huge fan of rainy days off. Nothing makes me happier than a day in pajamas, lounging around, watching the inclement weather with no place to go. I can lie around on my couch, food grazing and channel surfing all day long. Might seem boring to some and completely mindless, but sometimes it's just what the doctor ordered to turn everything off and recharge your creative batteries. I love horrible reality TV shows and sappy rom-com movies, and I can proudly recite every word to most of the Brat Pack movies of the '80s. I could watch the same movie a hundred times, and I aim to finish full seasons of a binge-worthy show in a day.

I'm married for more than half of my life to an amazing man who is fifteen years older than me. Getting married at twenty-four years old is not something I advise for most, but it happens to be one of the best decisions I ever made at such a young age. It doesn't work for many, but for me, it was truly meant to be. Joey is my biggest supporter, most important critic, moral compass, and most loyal fan. Skilled in construction as a career cement mason, he built our salon, and he's commonly known in our salon as *Schneider*, our trusty fixer of all things broken or in need of repair. His inappropriate sense of humor keeps us laughing all the time. Always willing to help out any way he can, it helps to cushion the stress I go through owning the business and doing the kind of creative work that I need to do.

We both decided a long time ago that we did not want to have children, which was a discussion we had and both agreed on from the time we started dating. You can call it selfish or closed-minded, but we think of it as honest. We travel a lot, both have hectic lives and work schedules, and we enjoy our downtime together with no interruptions. We fulfill our parental need with our dog, a Welsh corgi named Ella (and our other corgi Zoe, who passed a few years ago). I think the way we've molded our lives between work and play is just not something we felt we ever needed to do. We are surrounded by many nieces and nephews, and we are surrogate aunt and uncle to some of our friends' children. I love being an aunt because you get all of the love and do none of the work! And after all of these years, neither of us look back with any regret, feeling like we missed out on something.

I never really wanted kids. Even when I was a little girl, it wasn't something I dreamed of. Don't get me wrong. I do love kids, just someone else's kids. I had a great childhood. I value it too much as one of the hardest jobs a person could do and felt that if my whole heart was not into it, I shouldn't try. I assumed that one day, I might wake up and have that maternal ache, and to my surprise, it never happened. This might come across sounding selfish, but I think if I had children, I would possibly resent the fact that I couldn't put 100 percent in my career.

When my friends started building their families and began getting pregnant, I realized that I, too, craved the next stage of my life, but mine did not consist of diaper bags and strollers. I wanted to move on to my next chapter, and since becoming so unhappy in my work environment, I felt that I plateaued long enough working for someone else that it was time to venture into opening my own salon. As I opened my salon, my friends and I would commiserate about this new stage that we were all in. They would complain about the pains of new motherhood, and it was actually somewhat comparable to my new woes. They were up all night nursing and were exhausted from constantly tending to the baby, and my back was breaking from standing on my feet all day as I multitasked between cutting hair and fixing the clog in the shampoo sink. Listening to their cries, comparing them to my own, although they were on different playing fields, they seemed equally as overwhelming.

Although I had been in great health most of my life, I suffered a stroke a few years back, stemming from a heart defect I didn't know I had from childhood. Thankfully, the damage it caused reversed over time, and it didn't derail my career, but it did seem like it would at the time. A moment like that made me fear that I would lose the thing I loved the most—this crazy, dysfunctional career that took everything I had to build. It set me back for a while, and I had to limit my work and alter my schedule until this was under control. But that fear gave me the fuel I needed to get on top of this and the energy to fix what needed to be fixed so I can continue making the world pretty again as scheduled.

After two years of continuous transient-ischemic-attack stroke episodes—hallelujah—they finally figured out the problem, and I had heart surgery to fix it. Looking back now, I realize how lucky I am that this was possible. I had amazing support of my staff and family, a great surgeon/doctor, and I am beyond grateful that this health situation is finally behind me. Right after I had the surgery was when I realized how weak I had been for so long because my head was finally clear, my symptoms went away, and I felt great. And only as I write this and read back my words do I realize how absolutely nuts this sounds, but there I was, back behind the chair two days after having heart surgery. My heart was fixed, but I'm guessing I might actually be insane.

Work always came first. My friends learned early on that work took top billing and eventually learned how to navigate life without me. This led to my missing out on dozens of weekends away, last-minute ski trips and beach days. Soon, it parlayed into missing weddings, baby showers, christenings, communions, and special birthdays because I always chose work. In my early high school years, I used to travel with my alarm clock in the trunk of my car so if I stayed out late and slept out, I had to find an outlet to plug it in and set the alarm so I'd get up early enough to get to work on time in the morning. Some of my friends' parents were instrumental in getting me up early in the morning and got me to work on time while my friends slept till noon. Sounds tough to some, but I actually loved being at work. And besides, I always had money to buy the good quality beer, I made great connections to get us into the best clubs and bars, and I made enough money to furnish a great wardrobe that my friends would subsequently borrow when we went out on the town—after I teased and poufed their hair, of course.

But I do look back with some regret. I didn't allow myself the breaks to enjoy those special moments at my young age because I always "had to go to work." When I found myself left out from some special events, I would question why, and they would remind me, "We didn't think to invite you. We knew you had work."

I understood that growing a clientele and becoming successful at a young age wasn't easy, and it required that type of commitment, and I wouldn't have grown so much so quickly if I didn't. But looking back now, I feel like I cheated myself out of some good times, which might've made me a little less resentful as I got older. Those early years were so carefree and easy, yet there I was, working a full-time job with limited time to enjoy. Understandably necessary at the time, but it really hindered my social development, making me regretful as the years went on.

Let's start from the beginning. I always had an infatuation with hair. There wasn't a Barbie doll that was safe around me. I gave them all wacky bangs or painted highlights on their hair with Magic Markers. Born with a huge forehead, I had to wear bangs to help cover it up. My grandmother used her dull knitting shears to cut them on a regular basis. Having a huge mane of long hair, my mother would give me ponytails most days as my style or sometimes replaced the ponytail with the what she called the "Mork and Mindy," a "half up, half down" style with two pigtails on the crown of my head, fastening them with those old ponytail holders with the balls on the ends that even with all my skills, I still cannot figure out how to use.

The ponytail had to go by the time I was in fourth grade. As I matured into a sassy, foul-mouthed preteen, my mother would conveniently use my ponytail as a tool for punishment, not so gently pulling me by it when I cursed or rolled my eyes at her. I smartened up and opted for a stylish new shoulder-length unponytailed haircut, and I learned to roll my eyes when she wasn't looking.

My younger brother Doug was blessed with these beautiful curls on the top of his head, kind of resembling a Cabbage Patch doll. When my mother wasn't looking, I would sneak some scissors and trim it up. Of course, I would get in trouble, but after a while, she realized I was doing a pretty good job at it and would tell me, "I think your brother needs a haircut tonight. Let's give him one before he gets a bath."

My best friend Susan, who lived two doors down, had beautiful curly hair that people would be so jealous of. We were heading into junior high school, and I used her mother's old kitchen scissors to trim her hair before school started. It was at that moment that I discovered curly hair has a tendency to spring up and lay shorter than expected. Also, my novice hands couldn't quite master cutting an even straight line, especially with those god-awful scissors, so her lopsided hair became shorter and shorter, resulting in her midback-cascading curly hair turning into a sassy short, chin-length bob. She told me she loved it, but I secretly think she had to because she knew she was stuck with it. All in all, it turned out to be a great cut. Creating such a masterpiece in my eyes inspired me to be creative and make changes to help people look older, younger, prettier, different, or unique.

I decided to get a job in a hair salon when I was in the ninth grade. All of my friends were phenomenal athletes and were all occupied with sports after school. I went home each day bored out of my mind with nothing to do. Participating in sports was not my thing. I've never had an athletic bone in my body. So when I saw a sign at the salon where I got my haircut looking for a shampoo assistant, I figured it was the perfect job for me. It was in the neighborhood right up the block from the junior high school I was attending. The hours were after school and on weekends, so it would not to interfere with my school schedule. I would make some money, and it would keep me busy while my friends focused on their sport schedules. Partnered with my love of hair and my need to keep occupied, this was a match made in heaven!

I never anticipated how much I would love it and how inspired I would be each day from all that I would see and do. I became blind to any other career path, and I couldn't imagine doing anything else. My friends were all out on a ball field somewhere anyway, which I had no skill or interest in, so this kept me busy. This hair career found me, and it stems from my inability to catch, hit, or throw a ball. Lucky for my clients.

Many of my friends used to let me cut their hair in my garage. The guys were usually very trustworthy, and I would cut their hair with my stepfather's beard trimmer and an old pair of scissors that my boss gave me that he wasn't using. I became quite good at it, and all of that experimenting on them helped me understand how to actually cut hair properly from all the mistakes I made on their heads. Sidenote: my sincere apologies to anybody whose ears I've ever snipped or to the guys who had to walk around with a baseball cap on until their hair finally grew in. It was important to begin practicing and mastering precision cutting skills on people I knew, to help fine-tune myself on actual paying customers. And if I cut it too short? Hell, they weren't paying, so they were great guinea pigs to learn on!

Unfortunately, it's an important lesson to learn the right way to do something by doing it wrong and living with the consequences of the finished product. And till this day, I agree that everything that I do right, I have learned by screwing it up many times before. It has made me think twice or go about a strategy differently to ensure I give the client exactly what I promised. It's the thing I get praised for the most—my conservative approach—and it has helped me retain a huge client base throughout the years, allowing them to gain confidence and trust in my work.

It didn't always work out that way. There are many who left and never returned to my chair. Contrary to what many of my loyal clients would believe, there are actually many people in this world who would never let me touch their hair ever again due to pitfalls of my earlier learning years.

Stemming from my love of fashion, I always dressed older than I appeared. I used to borrow my mom's clothes to wear to work to look more sophisticated. The money I was making afforded me a great wardrobe, the Z. Cavaricci pants and Justin Boots I so desperately wanted. I loved working in the salon, dressed and feeling grown-up. I realized early on that looking good and being dressed nicely made people take you seriously. It shows that you care about what you looked like, and if you put effort into your own appearance, of course you would deliver the same to them. It made me fit in like the rest of the staff, and it helped me stand out to the clients. No one viewed me as some teenage kid pushing a broom in a salon. I was part of a glamorous team.

I loved being around people of all ages, learning about new styles and trends and products along the way. Early on, I displayed some skill, so I was invited to partake in some of the training workshops with the older girls in the salon. They allowed me to color, cut, and blow-dry their hair when they had time. I began cutting hair on actual clients in the salon when I was in eleventh grade, and my clientele quickly started to build. Some days, I would skip school after my morning cosmetology class was over to accommodate clients in the salon when needed. I was hooked. By the way, sorry, Mom. I believe the statute of limitations is up by now. Yes, your perfect daughter skipped school…all the time. But most of the time, it was to go cut hair at the salon. So does that actually equate to skipping school? It seems more like a work-study situation if you ask me. Whatever it was, I did it, and I loved it, and it worked.

Most of my work ethic comes from my grandfather Leo. He owned a butcher shop for years. I remember how dedicated he was to his job and how much of himself he gave to his business to succeed. He missed out on a lot to achieve that level of success, but the pride he had in it was admirable. He was my biggest supporter and was quick to defend me when others would criticize my career path, the long hours I worked, or my lack of college education. Poppy believed that the school of hard knocks was the best university and that a college degree, for many, was just a piece of paper in a frame.

He grew up without much, losing his parents during WWII in the Holocaust. He came to America at the age of twelve to start a new life, which he had to navigate on his own. I guess genetics played a big part in this because I understood it better than anyone else in our family could, and I walked his walk and talked his talk.

Owning a butcher shop since the early 1950s, he dealt mostly with women, who, at that time, were solely responsible for preparing meals for their hardworking husbands and families. He knew exactly how to schmooze the ladies, make small talk, and make them smile. He understood the art of taking care of people whether you agreed with them or not. That reputation is everything, and quality was key. He would visit me at the salon every day without fail. All of my clients looked forward to his visits to our salon to chat and have coffee with him, which he usually spilled all over the floor.

But whether I was hard at work on a client or mopping up his coffee mess, I always witnessed his proud face, watching me as

I worked, taking care of business. He saw himself in me. I hope he knew that I tried every day to be as good as he was. The salon was different after he passed, but his spirit stays with me. It's where I feel him the most. When I put my key in the door to open up each morning and say hello to his picture that we have displayed by our coffee bar, I think of him and try every day to keep his legacy alive.

I left my first salon after eleven years when I felt my career plateaued. I craved more. I wanted to expand my clientele and felt it was time. It was a scary moment going to work for a stranger after being with what felt like family for all of those years, but I felt in order to spread my wings, it was necessary. I learned a lot working for her. A lot of it was so different yet still the same. I succeeded in growing a bigger clientele, and it was great exposure to be the new girl in a bigger salon.

But as time went on, I knew in my heart this was not the place for me. As busy as I was, I felt the environment was toxic. The owner was nonexistent and took advantage of my workhorse ability. There is just so much one can take being the person responsible to bring in enough money to pay all the salon's bills and show up to run things smoothly while the owner is out on the town, neglecting the upkeep of the salon and conveniently forgetting to pay employees on time. If she'd been respectful enough to appreciate all the hard work that not only I but all of her employees did, I would've stayed working for her for a long time. Maybe I wouldn't have ever left, but the decision was ultimately made for me, and Karma played a big role in that.

Hairdresser Life

When I decided to write this book, I had so many thoughts running through my head that I felt it was time to start putting it all down on paper. So many years in this industry, watching so much begin to change that I have experienced what some would call the arc of a career. I'm still the same person standing behind a chair, essentially doing the exact thing I did from way back when I started yet evolving into a craft I never thought imaginable. The way I cut, the concepts of color, the world of hair extensions, and smoothing services are so different from the beauty-parlor life of lacquer and perms that I had entered into. I wonder if the fifteen-year-old Nikki could see what the fifty-year-old Nikki has become and saw the work I currently do, would she still want to become a hairdresser? Would it inspire her beyond her wildest dreams, or would it scare her into a different, more conventional path? I kind of think I'd wind up exactly where I am because this has been one hell of an exciting journey, and it proves that hard work does pay off.

As crazy as it all sounds, I do feel I was born to do this. I always worked well under pressure. Christmas shopping? I can get it all done three days before the holiday in two hours, wrapped and all. Big test tomorrow? Start studying the night before and cram in a month of notes onto study cards and somehow pass. So running a busy salon while working steady behind the chair over ten hours a day, five days a week? Piece of cake.

Now let's add in the ten to fifteen extra hours each week to do payroll, inventory, orders, bill paying, bookkeeping, creating social media content, and restocking everything we need for the new week—bigger piece of cake. Maybe ten years ago when I was younger…and not as wise. Thirty-five years of this has started to take its toll on me. I'm not as young as I was when I first started. My stamina has declined, my muscles hurt more, my brain can't keep up with my hands. The emotional trauma of the constant need of things to be addressed and fixed, the random fires to be put out on a daily basis—the reality sometimes hurts more than the actual pain I experience. A need for me to save face and not give in, to act as if I'm exactly as I was fifteen years ago—I challenge myself constantly to make it happen. It's seriously a case of self-abuse, a therapist's dream. If I had any extra free time, I'd start up a salon-owner support group because the burnout is real.

This industry can break you. Being a hairdresser is equivalent to being an actor on stage all day, every day.

- You have to be in a good, positive mood every day.
- You must be dressed professionally and try to look your best at all times.
- You have to be able to come up with a master plan on how to execute a miracle on the spot and somehow get it done in record time before the next client walks in.
- You must come up with creative ideas and help guide your clients who are indecisive and need help seeking a change.
- You must be a mind reader when they are trying to communicate what it is that they want. And you must communicate your interpretations right back to them so you are both sure you are on the same page.
- You must be calm and patient at all times, especially with those who show up late for their appointment.
- You must stay on time. Work at record speed to get it all done because the next client will be here any minute. And Lord knows no one wants to be kept waiting.
- You must be made of Teflon when clients are not happy with what you created, and be patient and helpful to turn that around.

- Like the deodorant ad says, "Never let them see you sweat." Do it all with the grace and ease of a seasoned, first-class flight attendant.
- Now go in your car and cry it out because no one needs to see you crack.

Now let's throw in owning the salon. Not only worrying about what you are doing in your chair but paying attention to every little detail that is happening in real time. Color stains on the chairs or all over the floor, backed-up laundry, overwhelmed front desk, stylists running behind schedule, an unhappy client in someone else's chair, working without the help of assistants, ticket pricing, back-ordered supplies, a light bulb out—I'm getting too old for this.

I dream about the days I worked for someone else, when I had a boss. Those were the good old days. I came in fifteen minutes before the first appointment and worked hard all day till the last client. Someone else paid me, provided me with all of my supplies, booked all of my appointments, they paid all the salon bills, and also took care of the management of the salon. And when I was done at the end of the day, scissors went down, blow-dryer put away, and I picked up my fancy pocketbook and left for the night. Those were the days.

Don't get me wrong. I wasn't the happiest while working for my last boss and even the boss I had before her. They were mostly absent, stingy with supplies, and very neglectful in their duties as a salon owner, which pushed me to make the decision to go out and do it on my own. I do what I do in my salon because they didn't. I make sure we are fully stocked with every bit of supplies that we need to successfully work through the day. I keep the salon in working order, fixing things that break and solving issues immediately. I try to keep harmony among the staff to have a positive work environment. I create inspiration and opportunity for my staff to retain a thriving salon culture. I am present for everything that happens at my salon even when I'm not physically there. I live, eat, sleep, and breathe my salon. And sometimes, it's exhausting. No, wait. Who am I kidding? Its fucking exhausting, and I'm now realizing why my last employer was as neglectful as she was. It's easier.

She never worried if we didn't have a shampoo assistant to help us out. She wasn't there to see us struggle, and to her, it was one less person to pay. Supplies? Who needs supplies? Figure out how to get a natural level 7 with a tube of level 5 and level 8! Payday? I'll pay them tomorrow or the next day; they can wait. Air-conditioning broke in September? Don't worry; the cool weather should be coming soon, so no need to fix it! Ah, the toilet is still broken? Go to the bar next door and use theirs; they don't mind! All bullshit! I'm not built like that. I didn't tolerate working that way back then; I couldn't bear the thought of doing that to my staff now. But, man, she was on to something. Being a responsible boss is exhausting.

Having that type of negative work environment fuels me to lead my salon in a functional, harmonious way. Nothing stays broken for more than twenty-four hours until "Schneider" (aka my husband, Joey) or a professional can get in to repair what needs to be fixed ASAP. Having to apologize to our clients at our former salon that the toilet was still broken since their last visit a month ago was embarrassing and, quite frankly not necessary, when all you need to do is call a damn plumber! Sure, it'll cost money, but a dysfunctional bathroom is not negotiable! If all of a sudden the air-conditioning isn't working properly, I better damn well be sure it gets fixed as soon as possible. No one wants to get their hair done while dripping in sweat. And it's even worse for the stylist. Just turning on the blow-dryer is equivalent to using a blowtorch in an un-air-conditioned environment.

Business ownership is a constant uphill battle. I've realized being a salon owner is equivalent to being a risk-management assessor. You must assume that something is going to break each day and be armed and ready to fix it, wrench or checkbook in hand.

What the hell did I know about owning a salon? This was a crash course in salon ownership, and I had no idea where to start. Although I didn't know much, I knew what *not* to do by my observation of my former employers. If I just did everything opposite how they did it, I'd be fine.

I was given great advice from a client who owned her own business. "Staff up," she said. "Surround yourself with people who can do for you what you can't do for yourself." If you don't know much about accounting or the financial end of running a business, get a good accountant. Not sure what products to supply? Build a relationship with your existing distributors and consultants, and they will guide you. It'll be tough keeping things clean and neat on a regular basis, so pay a weekly cleaning crew to help you out. Make sure your desk staff can handle all of the technical and economic issues to eliminate your stress. Be good to your employees so they wouldn't dream of working anywhere else.

As for staff employment, don't just settle on a subpar employee just because you can't find anyone else to do the job. Set them free, roll up your sleeves, and figure out a way to do it yourself if you have to. Lord knows if that puzzle piece is not fitting, it will never fit. Take pride in whom you hire, knowing that they are representing everything you've worked so hard for, allowing them to be part of your team.

Stick with what works, but be open-minded to new and easier ways of functioning in the workplace. Learn from every little thing that you disliked during your years of working for someone else and make it better. I made many mistakes along the way, and not everyone agreed with my way of business. I've bent over backward to keep my employees and my clients happy, but I've realized that is an impossible task, so I work to satisfy my own mission. So why mess with success and deviate my path? After eighteen years in business, it's a formula that has been proven to work. The clients are happy, and that is all that matters. I feel that I will not apologize for how I need to run my business. If you are not happy here, try being happy somewhere else. I'm sure you will see that their grass is not any greener than mine. It might even just be astroturf.

I'm not for everyone. My style of cutting or my color techniques might not be to everyone's liking, and after all of these years in the beauty industry, I've realized that's okay. I have a certain kind of finished look that I am known for, and it might not be favored by everyone. My colors are not overly edgy. I tend to specialize in more wearable-looking palettes. My blondes are subtle and lived in; my reds are vibrant but rich and natural looking. I don't favor unnatural neon hair color or stripy blonde highlights; my color work mimics natural hair color. My haircuts grow out nicely, and I favor light-weight products to allow hair to feel touchable and smooth.

My salon is friendly and chatty, where it sometimes feels like a big coffee klatch. I talk to each client *all day long*. My poor staff, they must hear my same stories over and over, but that's what my clients expect! They come in not only for their hair but to catch up on each other's lives. Some clients choose not to be serviced in that kind of environment; they would prefer to be incognito, read their book, and have a quiet experience, so they might not be a good fit for us, and that is okay.

When I started out, I thought I had to offer every single type of hair service there was, and take on work that I really didn't agree with in order to become successful, but, man, was I wrong. You can't be a restaurant that serves every kind of cuisine. You have to fine-tune your skills and put your energy into what you do best and what makes your heart happy. Just as it is in the fashion industry, some clothing styles are outrageously wild and trendy, and some are classic and sophisticated. You've got Betsey Johnson designing over-the-top patterns and risqué attire, and then there's Donna Karan showing classic designs and sharp silhouettes in relatable tones—both equally popular yet attracting a certain kind of audience.

I'm more like the latter. My clients love the consistency of my work. They value the naturalness of my hair color. The respectful way I guide them by knowing what has made them happy (or unhappy) in the past yet still helping them make changes to keep current, aware that if I do not feel I am capable of doing what they want me to do, I will gently decline and try to find them someone more qualified to get them there. I feel the mark of professionalism is refusing to do work that you know you can't do. You have their best interest at heart, and if you cannot get them to where they want to be, don't risk it.

One of the best compliments I've ever gotten is how clean and orderly my salon always is. Even coming back after COVID-19 lock-down, when cleaning protocols had to exceed all expectations, our clients told us that they had no doubt that we would have a healthy environment, knowing how clean we always were through the years. I have high standards regarding the cleanliness of my salon because I've worked in pigsties before, and I've heard the clients bitch about it. There is no excuse for filth and disarray. It's hard existing in our hairy environment to keep things clean at all times, but my team gets it done, and I think it's because they see me get on my own hands and knees right beside them and do it as well.

A clean work environment is a direct reflection of yourself, and being in an image-conscious industry, it's not negotiable. Clients expect and deserve a well-kept establishment. I run my salon as if Tabatha Coffey could walk through our door at any moment and inspect every detail. I equate our salon area to a dining room in a restaurant. Someone else has sat at this table before you, but when you sit down, it should appear as if no one occupied it at all. No crumbs from the last reservation, stained linens, dirty forks, or lipstick on the water glass. In our world, that means a clean station and tool area, a fresh haircutting cape, hair removed from the floor, no wet towels lying around, no drips of color on the seat, all shampoo residue wiped up from the shampoo sink, and any clumps of hair swiftly discarded from the sink drain.

It requires effort and consistency and becomes endless backbreaking work. It doesn't make the haircut any better, but it's what helps to make a reputable business. That's why they come back. Clients make a conscious decision to choose us, so of course it's our responsibility to keep things clean, making it a top priority to stay on our game.

Our job requires our full body to get the job done, not just our hands. Yes, of course our hands do all the work; they are our moneymakers. But our wrists move those hands around, and after a while, they ache, which leads to the forearms getting numb, elbows locking up, slouching and posture problems, ending in shoulder and neck pain, resulting in chronic headaches that never really go away. Years of chiropractic treatments, massage therapy, Icy Hot patches on your achy parts, and the constant use of Biofreeze or other topical remedies to get you through the day. After thirty-plus years, I've had to resort to getting spinal epidurals a few times a year to help alleviate the nerve pain in my collarbone that comes from a career working all day long with your arms up like a ballerina. Let's not forget those crippling midback spasms come from years of working while leaning forward with your arms at shoulder height. Trigger-point injections into the back muscles a few times a year temporarily takes care of that. Otherwise, you will spasm and freeze in that pose like the tin-man…with no oil can.

Many stylists suffer from carpal tunnel syndrome, forcing them to wear supportive wrist braces while working. Your hands go numb and ache all of the time. It hinders dexterity and gets worse with time. Eventually, some stylists have such extensive nerve damage and pain, they lose their ability to work and have to retire earlier than expected. Now *that's* just the upper body.

Lower back pain is very common in our industry, enduring years of standing all day long, usually on hard floors. Even more so if you don't wear the best foot attire—guilty as charged. I'm speaking for myself, but I swear I work better in heels. Sciatica pain starts in the hip joint and begins shooting down your legs as the day progresses. So that's when you apply one of those big Icy Hot or Salonpas patches to your lower back to numb and soothe that flaming lumbar to get you to your last client of the day.

Moving down to the lower extremities—leg pain, blood clots, chronic knee lock, varicose veins, ankle swelling, aching feet (even *with* good, supportive shoes), numbness on the ball of the foot, clicking ankles, arthritic toes, bunions, plantar fasciitis, ingrown toenails. And let's not forget how swollen our feet get from just simply standing all day. You name it, we get it. Our legs are like a train caboose, supporting all our weight, keeping us vertical as we put in six, eight, ten, twelve hours days. By the end of the day, our legs feel like tree trunks as we crawl out to our cars to finally sit for probably the first time that day.

The work we do is extremely physical, and we trick you all by making it look easy. Just the other day, after my assistant blew out two clients in a row, she told me that her shoulders hurt, and her wrist was aching from all that hard work, that she cannot believe we do this all day with no problem. I'm more than twice her age, and I'm physically working on ten to fifteen clients a day without breaking a sweat. Two blowouts, and she's ready to throw in the towel!

On to the mental capacity one needs to remain calm and focused behind the chair, our personal life is left out in the parking lot when we enter the salon each day. Our own personal issues should never be the client's problem. If we had a fight with our spouse, it will be dealt with after work because Mrs. Jones needs to get her roots done, and we need to stay focused to get Rebecca's hair done on time for her Bat Mitzvah. Even if I've received bad news on the phone while at work, I take a minute to process and then put it in the back of my mind while I focus on the job in my chair. Sometimes that's a better way to help deal with stress—walk away from it for a bit and occupy yourself with something else. Our issues will be out there double-parked all day in the parking lot, where it will remain until we are focused and ready to handle it.

In order to succeed in this career path, you must be able to build up an invisible callous, a tough shell that will be able to protect you from negative feedback. If you accidentally cut your client's bangs a bit too short, or they seem unhappy with the new highlights you gave them, yes…they are going to be a little unsatisfied. But you can't curl up and die and implode into an emotional mess because your client was unhappy. I've seen it too often to count. A client comes in with a minor complaint, and afterward, the stylist is locked in the bathroom in a puddle of self-doubt.

The thing we need to realize is if the client was truly unhappy with your work, she wouldn't be back to complain to you. She would just go somewhere else for her services. She's simply letting you know so you don't do that the next time. Her devotion to you as a stylist should build your confidence that her gripe was just a gentle reminder, not a need for a Xanax and a career change. My assistant recently told me that her biggest fear was a client not loving her work and that it was the reason she was afraid to move up and work on clients behind the chair as a stylist. You can't think that way. Without building up a tough exterior and choosing to have a negative attitude, you will never grow. You need to put on your big-girl/boy panties, take full responsibility, and do whatever you can to make them happy.

I've always felt that if your client isn't happy with your work, yet they came back to you, albeit with a complaint, you did a good job building a solid relationship with them. It shows that they really love you, will not leave you over this, and trust that you will stand behind your work and do whatever it takes to satisfy their needs. To fall into a full-blown anxiety attack about it is completely unnecessary. You grow from these experiences and learn to be more cautious the next time you work on their head. It's a task that is definitely easier said than done. It comes with experience and time. And a little Pinot Noir helps too.

We build tremendous anxiety trying to compartmentalize our own lives and focus on what you need. And in a matter of minutes, we need to come up with a master plan on how to get your colored dark-brown hair to soft-blonde balayage in two hours…while silently praying that it comes out to your liking because if you are not happy, we will spend the next few sleepless nights beating ourselves up, thinking about how we could've done it differently. It's part of the job, but it's much tougher than we make it look and all while being consistent enough to remember every detail of your life, staying on time to execute your desired miracle, all while having a positive attitude and a smile on our faces. I dare you to try it. We make it look easy, but boy, it is not.

That's the thing that I think clients don't realize. How our body struggles to keep up with our mind, which needs to keep up with our hands, all while staying on our schedule with a happy, positive demeanor—all to make you happy. Trust me, we love to do it. Your happiness is our goal because the best advertisement is a happy client.

But it comes with a price. We are supposed to make it look easy. If we panic, you panic, so we smile and make casual chitchat about the weather, talk recipes, or discuss reality TV to distract you from the physical pain we are in or the anxiety of the task or our need to pee.

Speaking of which, do you know that hairdressers have the highest risk of getting a UTI? Once we start a three-hour highlight service, there's no time to stop, especially since we might've already started a few minutes late. We need to keep the application timing perfectly so it all processes at the same time. And when you are busy all day long with back-to-back clients, there is no time to stop. And you can bet that when we have that two-minute window of opportunity to use the bathroom, someone is definitely going to be in there!

It is also a sad fact that approximately three out of every five hairdressers suffer from anxiety disorder. Our existence behind the chair is to be constantly on, being creative and punctual in both physical and mental ways. The days are long, and the demands are high. No one comes in and wants to hear if we are having a bad day. We need to act as if everything is okay even if it's not. It takes brainpower and a coat of armor to accomplish each head and the problems we face with each client. And the simple task of "fake it till you make it" backfires when the day is over, and we are left to process it all. Exhausted and depleted of energy, sometimes it feels like our lives don't matter because we are always putting others first…just to do it all again tomorrow. Just writing about this is giving me anxiety.

Selfishness does not exist with our type of career. I've sacrificed my own happiness and planned my personal events so not to coincide with busy seasons at the salon. I purposely got married in March because it's a quiet time before the Easter-Passover chaos begins. I had to quit cheerleading in high school because I was needed at the salon on the weekends. I arranged surgery so I would be back to work in time for the busy holiday season. Couldn't plan a vacation if I had a bride I committed to take care of on a specific weekend.

Stylists have missed their kids' recitals, multiple first days of school, and special events because we are expected to show up for the task and will be crucified if we disappoint. We are expected to put everyone else's lives before ours and celebrate their joys when it is good for them even if it coincides with something important for us. Always up at the ass crack of dawn to beautify the bride yet getting dressed and doing our makeup in the car on our way to attend their wedding. Always toting along a bag of tricks to fix anything hair related that she or another guest might need throughout the day, missing most of the cocktail hour because we are on duty in the bridal suite.

It feels like our lives are secondary to the needs of our clients. It's not brain surgery, but we are a very important component in people's lives, and we are expected to create when it is good for them, and after a while, we feel secondary. I wouldn't do it if I didn't think the person in question didn't appreciate it, but sometimes it feels expected more than it should.

Oftentimes, the burnout that hairdressers face can cause physically challenging situations to our health. Having had a stroke a few years ago made me realize what a gift it is to have your hands, head, and body work like clockwork without even thinking about it. I was fortunate that my stroke did not cause paralysis or impair my ability to use my hands, but brain fog set in, and my speech and word finding was slightly affected, so I had many moments where my hands, brain, and mouth weren't on the same page. I learned how to calm myself and slow my roll, allowing myself time to get it all in sync to take care of each client in my chair. Taking more time to do a task was foreign to me because I usually can juggle two to three clients at a time but proved to be most effective during that period.

The panic of my own health, both physically and mentally changing in a way that could've caused me to stop working for good, made me take a step back to focus on my recovery to get better. I aimed to get more sleep each night, eat healthier, work out sensibly to keep my body strong, and start to de-escalate my work capacity. Lucky for me, my stroke did not derail my career, and I begin every day realizing how fortunate I am that I can still do it. It makes you realize that nothing in life is for sure, and you never know what tomorrow will bring. Health issues can happen to anyone at any time, and no one is exempt from that. And if you don't have your health, you have nothing.

Risky Business

It's important to have very sharp scissor blades in our arsenal to perfect our haircuts. Dull blades tear at the hair and cut unevenly, leaving us with unblendable lines and a poorly defined style. So in order to stay on top of our cutting game, it is important to service our sheers regularly. But one false move with those sharp blades and it's a possible trip to the ER. They are surgically sharpened and dangerous if we accidentally over snip.

It can be a little cut or, in some cases, like an episode of *Law & Order: Special Victims Unit*. Snipping our skin is a constant occupational hazard, and unfortunately, we have to swiftly tend to it and get right back in the game. The last thing you want to do is let your clients know that you just sliced half your finger open while working on their head, so you calmly make an excuse to remove yourself for a second, then you hightail it to the back room, where you assess the damage.

Any good salon keeps everything you need for these situations... peroxide, Band-Aids, those condom-looking finger cots, and yes, Krazy Glue. Krazy Glue, or in my salon medical kit, quick-drying nail glue and nail resin setting spray are used to seal up the cut so no hair or debris can get in. Once you get the bleeding under control and sanitize it to be sure it's clean, we apply the glue over the cut, set it with nail glue setting spray, apply a Band-Aid along with a finger condom, and it's back to business as usual. And for those who are cringing to hear that I put glue on an open cut, FYI: Krazy Glue is actually used in lieu of stitches in Third-World countries. It is nontoxic, and trust me, I've used it so many times in my career, and

I'm still here with all ten fingers to tell the story. But like most occupational hazards, it's par for the course in the hairdressing industry.

From cut scars to iron burns, our hands are like road maps. Teflon hands, I refer to them as. I've personally cut myself so many times in my career on certain spots that I don't bleed as much due to the scar tissue that has built up due to multiple cuts over the years! Only recently since I had the stroke, I am on blood thinners as a precaution, which makes even a paper cut bleed without fail. The slightest of grazes with the blade, and it's like an scene from *American Horror Story*.

I cut myself so badly early in my career that I almost cut the entire skin off the knuckle of my left middle finger. I had a chatty client in my chair who always turned her head to face up at me when she was talking, and after correcting her ten times to talk to me by looking at me in the mirror, she turned yet again, and it happened. As I snipped, I saw the blood, and I realized the damage was done. Not to alarm her or hurt her feelings, I smiled and said, "Give me a second. I'll be right back," and ran into the separate nail department of the salon to rinse it in their sink and assess how bad it actually was. And boy, it was brutal, a deep V-shaped gash on my knuckle joint.

My nail technician friend Gina ran to me, knowing what the problem might be, and helped me. She stopped the bleeding with her styptic drops, glued it down, and bandaged it up good, but it wasn't going to help. Due to the deep cut on the knuckle, I wouldn't be able to bend my finger; otherwise, the bleeding would start all over again. Like MacGyver, Gina broke an emery board in half, and like a splint, she put it on the underside of my finger and taped my finger securely to it to stop it from bending. We cleaned up the remnants of the massacre in the sink. I took a deep breath, and returned to my client. I continued to finish her haircut and somehow blow it out.

Funny enough, she never realized why I went missing, nor did she recognize the huge taped-up middle finger I had awkwardly used to complete her hair. She was so chatty with everyone else around her, she hardly noticed I was gone! It was smack in the middle of a busy Saturday, and my clients were beginning to pile up, so I forged forward and completed four more haircuts before I left to go to the hospital for stitches.

A few years back, I cut the right side tip of my pointer finger completely off. It was a foolish move on my part. I was working quickly to stay on schedule, too busy talking, and oops! The client saw me do it, but I acted like it was no big deal. I put my scissors down, smiled as I excused myself, and casually walked away then scurried to the back room to assess the damage. Some of my hairdressers followed me back there, knowing by the look on my face what it was. As I was rinsing, and holding pressure on it. I realized the skin was actually missing. Sometimes when you cut yourself with scissors, it's like a deep V that leaves a flap that could be eventually sealed down. Not in this case. It was clearly sliced off.

One of the hairdressers quietly retrieved my scissors from my work station and found the cut skin still on it. At this point, there is no way to reattach it, and there was no way to stitch this closed. She went back out to finish up the cut for me as I tended to this mess. Peroxide, styptic drops, glue, more glue, glue spray, Band-Aids, finger condom. Walked out of the back room like Miss America. "Oh, this? It's just a little cut. No big deal." I had it wrapped so tightly that the pain wasn't so bad. It was holding up okay. I had it bandaged up pretty well, so I did what any idiot would do. I stayed and finished the rest of the day.

I had a young assistant helping us unpack a delivery of products, and she accidentally cut herself with the knife she was using to open the boxes. Once she saw the blood, she turned sheet white, her eyes rolled back, and she almost fainted. I advised her that this haircutting career might not be the best decision for her because there was no way she could avoid this in the future if she planned on working with scissors.

At a hairstyling workshop many years ago, we were being taught fancy updos and new curling techniques. They supplied us with mannequin heads, the hair products from their line, and curling irons for us to use, which happened to be Marcel irons. Marcel irons are a specific type of curling irons meant for professional use only. They are designed without a safety tip to grab on to in case you needed some support while curling. They are hotter than most irons, and you have to be well seasoned to use one. Well, one spin with the iron, and I got myself good with the hot tip on the side of my pointer finger and then again on my thumb. Two blisters appeared immediately and took almost two weeks to go away. Needless to say, I couldn't participate in the curling portion of that class. Those two little burns caused so much pain, it was agonizing. And even though this happened years ago, I still have a faint scars from that day. At least when I cut off the tip of my pointer finger that I just spoke about, it lobbed off the area where one of those scars resided. See? Silver lining!

All splinters suck, but unless you've ever gotten a hair splinter, you will never know how painful they are. A wood splinter or any other foreign material is more visible to the naked eye. Hair splinters are microscopic and get embedded in the skin without any visible trace…until you feel them. It's equivalent to walking on glass. I've had them so deep in the pad of my feet, that I would feel it before I could ever see it. It takes forever to get out, but the minute you do, a rainbow appears in the sky, the birds chirp happily, and the pain instantly goes away. I have actually gotten a hair splinter in my bra. Oh, Jesus, the agony. And it's always the first customer of the day—you know, the lady with the really coarse curly hair. So all day long, you feel it going places it doesn't belong. It's important to check every part of your body at the end of the day and to wipe out the insides of your shoes for any remnants of cut hair. Just thinking about it, I'm itchy.

I've gotten color in my eye, my mouth, up my nose—you name it—an occupational hazard that you just get used to. I've successfully foiled an entire head of highlights with one eye closed because I flicked a speck of bleach in my eye. The client had no idea. I carried on a conversation and expertly finished without missing a beat. Finished result was the same as it ever was. Safe to say, I didn't die from it. I'm here to tell the story.

I've stained every article of clothing that I've ever worn to work with bleach or hair dye. Color on your white jeans? Just use a little leftover hair bleach on it; comes out like it never happened. Bleach spots on my black shirt? A dab of dark hair dye does the trick. And if not, sharpie marker to the rescue—works every time.

It takes a lot to sway a stylist—cut finger, hair splinter, toxic chemicals in your eye. Hairdressers are superheroes. Nothing stops us.

Beauty School Dropout

For a long time, the hairdressing industry was looked down upon as a peasant occupation, a job you resorted to because you weren't smart enough to get into college. When I was in high school working as an assistant, a client asked what colleges I planned on applying to. I explained that I wasn't planning on going to college once I graduate high school. I planned to work full-time and focus growing my career as a hairstylist. He looked at me with disappointment and had the nerve to ask, "Do you want to be known as just a hairdresser for the rest of your life?"

Little did he know, at seventeen, I was making more money than he was at my part-time, after-school job, yet he had a cute little diploma on the wall of his cubicle at his office job, so he felt he was on a better life track than me. The idea of college wasn't something I felt I needed to entertain, but if I really wanted to go, I damn well would've. I chose to favor this career path, investing my time building myself in this beautiful industry, making people happy every day. College isn't for everyone. Just because you get a college degree doesn't mean you have your life paved out for you. As my grandfather always said, "A degree is just a piece of paper. You're going to wake up every day and go to work. Make sure it's something you love." So I did.

It's not a field for rejects, a purgatory for those who can't find themselves. It's not for the weak or the unmotivated because if you do not have the heart, it won't work. It's backbreaking work, partnered with a street-smart sense of how to deal with the public. Trying to analyze what the client is asking you to accomplish and requiring the stamina to do it, finding the strength to stay patient, while maintaining the ability to consistently create.

A friend of my mom became my client. She was interested in having her daughter take the cosmetology course that was offered in her high school. She asked for my advice and guidance because she had questions regarding my career path. Her daughter was a bratty, unmotivated sixteen-year-old, whose parents did everything for her. I personally experienced the young girl's lazy behavior and blatant disrespect toward her parents in social situations. The mom began to explain that her daughter's grades were poor, and they were afraid she wouldn't even be accepted into a college, so they figured hairdressing was a good fallback for her.

While speaking with her, I realized she was under the impression that I must've been financially supported by my parents and now by my husband, whom she referenced had a "real job." She asked if I was single, would I possibly be able to support myself with a career in this field? As if I did this as a hobby! She clearly looked down at a career in hair, assuming it was a last-resort career path for dummies until you finally met someone to pay your bills.

I surprised her by explaining that I made more money that year than my husband did, that the house I live in, the car I drive, and the life I live are all thanks to my hair career. How much money you can make is up to the stylist. It depends on how much you're willing to put into your craft. You work hard, you make a lot. You slack off, you stay on Mommy and Daddy's payroll. This is not a fallback career. This career path requires talent, drive, and passion. I really did not see any potential or passion in her daughter to try to help or mentor her. Plus, I was really offended that she thought so poorly of this amazing industry and clearly of me.

I still sense a hesitation at times when I tell certain people that I am a hairdresser. It's a shame that some people are so closed-minded that if you don't have a college degree, they place you into a different category. I found myself at a swanky country club, surrounded by wealthy doctors, corporate executives, and the upper echelon of Long Island's North Shore. We were invited to dinner by a friend of my husband who belongs there. I love any reason to dress up, and I had a sense of how to look to fit in with this crowd.

In conversation with the wives, one of them asked what I do for a living, and when I explained that I was a hairdresser, they exchanged glances and stared at me for a bit, probably wondering why on earth I would be joining *them* for dinner. One of the ladies replied, "That is so great! The world needs hairdressers, you know." Well, the world needs ditchdiggers too. I guess I see where I stand with this crowd. Instead of saying I was a hairdresser, I should have probably rephrased it and told them that I make people happy…every damn day. Tell me what other occupation can do that? I am proud of what I do, and I'd like to see them walk a day in my shoes. They'd probably send their nanny to do it. Too beneath them to resort to such manual labor. Let's see how they feel when they can't get in for a hair appointment. I bet they'd think more highly of me than…

When The Shit Hits The Fan...

I've worked through three recessions, a global pandemic, devastating hurricanes, and endless record-screeching moments throughout my career. But the one thing I recognize is that throughout any situation, everyone wants to look good…and to feel normal.

Through recessions, when most people were conserving money, they had to do without the things that at one time were normal necessities but in tough financial times became a luxury. No vacations, less restaurant dining, far less shopping sprees. But getting a different haircut or a change to your hair color was an inexpensive quick fix to make you look and feel good. And in a sense, looking good makes life seem normal. You might not be jetting off to some exotic vacation, but when you look in the mirror, you see something new that made you happy. It doesn't break the bank to get a new haircut or add a few highlights, and it's much cheaper than a fancy new outfit, vacation, or expensive dinner out in a restaurant. Looking good is a luxury to some, but it is a necessity to many. And like the old saying goes, when you look good, you feel good.

We were lucky enough to survive through Superstorm Sandy, a devastating hurricane that created tremendous damage to most of the New York area. Almost everyone in our area lost power and had unfixable damage done to their houses. Most people were displaced from their homes due to flooding, damage from fallen trees, and loss of electricity. Surprisingly, even though most everyone around us were affected by the outages, our salon never lost power. When the storm was over, we drove to the salon, wondering what shape we were going to be in, and to our surprise, the lights went on, and we were fine.

Well aware how many people were unfortunately suffering from the aftermath, we posted to our social media channels to invite clients to come visit our salon. We welcomed them in to have their hair washed, use our Wi-Fi, have coffee while charging their phones or devices, or to simply escape their cold, powerless houses. These people were dealing with so much already; it only made sense to pay it forward to our loyal clients. Nothing feels better than having your hair washed to begin with, but in a time when all you have at home is cold water and no electricity, to them, it felt like we gave them a million dollars. We set up a self-service station equipped with hair products, a blow-dryer, and brushes for clients to dry their hair themselves. Most had homes that were demolished in the storm and had no idea where they were going to live or when life would be back to normal again. So we provided a place of comfort to humanize with clean hair, friendly people, and a cup of coffee while you charged your devices…and your soul.

When asked where they were when some of life's worst or memorable moments occurred, many clients can say they were with me. Where were you when Michael Jackson died, when OJ was being chased, during the East Coast summer blackout of 2003? Many were with me in my chair, and we talk about it till this day.

But I cannot think of the morning of September 11 and not see the faces of the clients who were there with me that day. We listened closely to the details from the salon radio, hugging each other and crying as the events unfolded. They came in like robots because that's what they had scheduled for that day, but I really think they came, knowing they would be with a friendly face, which would be comforting at that horrible moment in time. At that moment, no one cared about their hair, but the simple task of being there to get their hair done made this surreal time feel somewhat normal, and that's what everyone needed to feel to get through that day and the weeks after.

And let's not forget one of the worst times in our history, the shutdown of COVID-19. I never thought in a million years that this unknown virus affecting China would cause the shutdown of life across the globe as it did. Looking back now, it is surreal to think every business, every school, every family went into a quarantine state in a flash. Patients alone in the hospitals and in nursing facilities. Lines outside supermarkets limiting how many people could enter. Masks on our faces and gloves on our hands to be anywhere in public. Teachers, students, and parents having to learn overnight how to navigate school learning via computer. Constant fear of catching this unknown virus and what it will do to you if you got it. And as for my clients, they were in a panic that their secret would soon be revealed, wondering what to do about their gray roots.

Our hair-color line Tocco Magico is imported from Italy, so when the virus spread and Italy went into a lockdown, I feared that it might be difficult for me to restock my color when I would need it later that year. Never thinking we would be shut down, knowing that the color has a pretty long shelf life and would eventually be used, I ordered a ridiculous amount of color just to be safe. And then it happened. There we were—salon shutdown, no idea when we would reopen, with seventeen huge cardboard boxes full of expensive unopened color sitting in every room of my house…and a bill for it all waiting to be paid.

Floods of texts were coming my way from clients, asking what type of box dye I could recommend for them to use during our time closed. I conferenced my hairdressing staff, and they were experiencing the same panicked inquiries from their clients. Our fear was aside from not knowing what to recommend, we would be inundated with having to perform corrective color on the botched jobs that they would have from using unknown box dye. And knowing how limited our availability would be with everyone wanting to come in as soon as we opened, we would have no time to help everyone.

Looking at those stacks of boxes filled with color, the light bulb went on. What about hair-color kits? If we put together a small mixture of each client's personal color formula with all the tools for them to apply themselves, it would be a much-better option for clients than one of those toxic, questionable box dyes. We advertised on social media that we were offering customized hair-color kits for our existing clients, and *boom*—overnight success!

I couldn't keep up with the orders, and I've never seen people so happy to do their own hair color in my life! Clients would put in an order for a kit, and we would go in early on the day of pickup and put together a mixture of their own color formula. The kit included a color-applicator brush, gloves, protective stain cream, color-remover wipes, comb, a plastic cap, and how-to directions. I even made a video of myself coloring my own hair as a tutorial to teach clients how to do it themselves.

The day of pickup was like a well-orchestrated drug deal. Clients would text us once they arrived in our parking lot, and we would bring out their kit. They'd pop the trunk; we'd drop it inside; they slip an envelope of money out of their window and drive away. My husband would stay parked in his car as a form of security while this transaction would take place, shaking his head at the insistence of our clients to get their hair color. The whole world was coming to an end, but they needed their gray roots covered! And the truth is, they did.

Life was so upside-down for everyone for all different reasons. They were either working from home, monitoring home schooling, not working, home all alone, home with too many people, away from life and their loved ones, stressed out, not knowing when or if life would get back to normal again. And when they'd wake up in the morning and brush their teeth, they would look in the mirror and see that dreaded skunk line and start their day off depressed. If their grays were gone, at least when they would look in the mirror, they'd see a better version of themselves and start their day off right.

It made clients appreciate us even more, realizing firsthand that although we make it look easy, how difficult a task it actually is to do. And to my delight, it provided an activity for kids and spouses, some of whom helped take part in applying the color, learning a new skill at the same time! They would send funny pictures and videos of their process being done and be so grateful for our help and support.

What we did with those color kits was provide a connection to our clients to show them that although we weren't able to do it for them, this was an extension of us to them. It kept us relevant to our clients and showed that we still cared. Through the years, our clients have become family to us, and providing this service for them only made us closer. And when we were able to reopen, everyone came back. They were patient with our protocols and limited availability and were supportive, understanding, and happy to have us back.

I've never spent much time away from work. I took two weeks off when I got married, but that was a rarity. We were closed eleven weeks due to COVID-19 lockdown. I learned a lot about myself in that time and took on a different perspective about my chosen career. I realized that I am fueled by people. I see a different person every thirty minutes in my chair, and during that time away from work, I missed that connection the most. I've given so much of myself to my clients that I didn't know what to do with all of this stagnant time off. I didn't know what purpose I could serve in life if I couldn't be behind the chair. It made me realize that I have no finish line as to when I will be done doing hair. I will never retire from this field. Of course, I will not be working the same crazy schedule as I do now, but I envision myself in my late eighties as that hip old lady, hopefully still in heels, working in the salon.

I've given babies their first haircut and then, years later, have done their hair for their prom and even eventually their weddings. Hell, I've even given *their* kids their first haircuts. Hard to believe I've been at this so long, but it's true. And I'm still standing. It's not common to last this long in this industry, to watch babies grow into functioning adults and then some. A seven-year-old client never thought I'd make it this far. She had come to only me her entire young life but requested to have her haircut with one of my younger stylists instead. When her mom questioned why, she replied, "Nikki's been doing this a long time, and Krista is much younger. When I graduate high school and get married, I'm not sure if Nikki will still be doing hair then, but I am pretty sure Krista will."

How fucking old did she think I was? I guess she thought by the time she'd be graduating high school, I'd be in a nursing home down in Boca Raton or even worse, dead. She is currently twenty-three years old, still a client, and I am still vertical and functional, to her surprise! And when her *young* stylist had to go out on maternity leave, guess who had to step in and do her hair? That's right! Me,

Grandma Moses! This old lady still had it in her, and we laugh about this all the time. Her perception at that young age was that it would be better to build a relationship with a younger stylist because they would have more longevity to be there for her the long run. Little did she know, I am the Timex of hairdressers, the immortal stylist that keeps on ticking.

Sadly, not all of my client experiences are joyful. I've held their hands during their illness diagnosis, counseled them through break-ups and divorce, and cried with them at the loss of family members and pets. Through the relationships we build, we become part of their inner circle and become a stoic rock for them to lean on. It means more to me to know that they trust me enough to lean on me to be part of their team.

One of my clients snuck me in through his window at his rehab facility when they told him he couldn't have someone come in to cut his hair. Always a rule breaker, he insisted I come anyway. I quickly cut his hair and cleaned him up, and it made his day. He had been bedridden for a few weeks but needed a pick-me-up, and the haircut did the trick. No one found out I was there, and it made him so happy to get away with this caper. And I left the same way I came in—through the window!

I've helped many through their cancer treatments and have cut their hair at nursing homes, at their home, or in the hospital when they were too ill or frail to come to the salon. I feel that if I could be with them for the good, it is my duty to be with them through the bad. Nothing brings a bigger smile to a person's face than a fresh haircut or to have their hair blown out when they are in a hospital. To look good somehow makes you feel better.

An older client of mine had broken her leg and was house-bound due to her injuries. She was devastated that she couldn't walk around her house and had to sit around all day in a recliner. She was even more devastated that she couldn't come to the salon for her weekly blowout appointment! Twice a week for the six weeks that she was immobile, I went to her house to wash and blow out her hair. Washing her hair was no easy task. We had to shift her body around to hang her head over the side of the recliner as I poured warm water from a pitcher into a garbage pail. But when it was done, and she felt pretty again, it was worth all the effort because she felt normal even if it was just from the neck up.

When someone is losing their hair due to chemotherapy, I would never allow them to go through that alone. It's not an easy thing for me to do, but in that moment, it's not about me. We do it together in a quiet, dignified setting so they are comfortable having their hairdresser take care of them in that tense moment. I will adjust the cut on their wigs if needed and show them how to style it. And when their hair begins to grow back in, I'm right there to help them through the stages. It's a very emotional time for them, but I help them every step of the way.

To me, it's one of the most important tasks I could ever be asked to do. I can't do much to make them physically healthy, but I can definitely help them with their mental and emotional health, to help them at a time when they are going through the most unthinkable situation of their lives. When they are scared, feeling ugly, and feel so unlike themselves, it's your duty to be there. We touch lives. It's not just about making them look like a model in a magazine. We help make them look and feel normal, and for them, it's priceless…and to me too.

The Dark Days Of Covid-19

What a blur, a big, ugly, stressful, scary moment in time. How easy is it to contract? Will we die if we get it? How long will my business be shuttered? Will we ever reopen? Will we ever be normal again? I sound like any human who lived through COVID-19 in the spring of 2020.

Like everyone else in our world, I never thought in a million years that our lives would be so affected by this weird virus spreading through China. Then it was in Italy, then all of Europe. We heard about eight cases in the US, some on the West Coast, then the East Coast, than cruise ships were not able to dock, with passengers stuck, quarantined on the boat due to fear of spreading from a few affected passengers. It all began to feel real.

I figured we would follow a rigid sanitary protocol in the salon, Clorox wipe all surfaces and space out the amount of clients at a time, all while still continuing to make the community beautiful. Then we ran out of Clorox wipes, then Lysol, then hand sanitizers, then, for what reason I still have no idea, toilet paper, proving that someone must know the truth, that the end of the world was near.

When there was word that we would be shut down, at first, I laughed it off, then I realized the severity of the situation coming closer to home and figured maybe at the worst, we would shut down for a week or so, let the dust settle, and it'll be back to business as usual. I remember it so clearly—leaving work at the end of the day on Saturday, March 14, walking out to the parking lot with three other employees. I recall telling them that this would all blow over and that we would work like normal the following week. That next day was bright and seasonally warm, so I went for what I thought would be a nice walk in my neighborhood, only to commiserate on all of my neighbors' driveways that the floodgates have opened, and things were rapidly shutting down. By Monday, everyone was in panic mode, and I had no choice but to join the club.

I called my three hairdressers and worked out a plan for all of us to work in shifts the next day, safely accommodating as many of that week's scheduled clients because the rumor of a shutdown was happening. We were open that Tuesday for fourteen hours, each of us taking turns working in shifts so not to overload the capacity in the salon. When we locked up that night, I thought we would probably stay closed for a few days and worked out a schedule to reopen by the weekend. I came to work on Thursday by myself to accommodate a few clients, but by Friday, we were in full-mandated lockdown.

Long supermarket lines, no paper towels or toilet paper, *Tiger King* on Netflix, baking banana bread, and this weird obsession with sourdough bread—whatever got us through that time, we were all in it together. Thank God the liquor stores were deemed essential, so they were left opened. Gray roots became the biggest problem for most of my clients, so for fear that they would buy box dye on Amazon, we decided to launch our customized hair-color kits for our existing clients. It would be easier in the long run if we supplied them with our own color, which, if mixed by us, would be easier to correct than box dye. Then their friends and neighbors were on to their secret and wanted in, so we started formulating color kits for strangers via photos that they would text us.

All of the years I lived in my neighborhood, not knowing anyone due to my usual hectic work schedule, I now became the most popular person in my area. I was now known as "the hair-color girl," coloring everyone in my town. No one really needed it for professional reasons; it was strictly emotional. We were all miserable, distant from our loved ones, stuck in the house. But goddamn it, if they got rid of those gray roots, they could get through their time in purgatory.

Some salons refused to participate in making color kits for their clients. They stood their ground that they were unique hair-color artists, and what they do behind the chair was magic, and they wouldn't subscribe to a client feeling like they can do it themselves. Fuck that! In a moment like this, all a client can see is their growing roots and the truth serum of their gray percentage. They don't give a shit at that moment how unique and special you are as a hair artist. Help them to cover their roots—that's all they care about!

And the sad truth for a lot Michelangelo's clients, they were annoyed that their colorist wouldn't support them at this time of need and never returned to them once lockdown was over. They got color kits from me to satisfy the problem at hand, chose to stay with us as clients, and always remembered that their pompous hair artist didn't care enough to bend the rules for them.

It was a dark time for me personally. I realized with all of this time not working that I was a workaholic. And like a drug, I craved the presence of people. Some days, I'd wake up at 7:00 a.m. and force myself to go back to sleep until ten because that would be three less hours that I didn't have to worry what to do with myself.

I'd wake up late morning, go out for a long walk, and plan out what our menu would be for the day. My rule was to wait until the clock said p.m. to start my first cocktail of the day. Walk, eat, drink, nap, watch TV, repeat. Before you know it, it'd be 10:00 p.m., a season or two of whatever Netflix show you were watching was over, and tomorrow, you would do it all over again.

And then I broke my foot. FML. Stupid really. I think I'm just destined to be standing all day in heels behind a chair because three weeks walking around barefoot in my house is how I did it. I got up in the middle of the night to pee, and it rolled out from underneath me, and *bam!* Jones fracture. I broke the fifth metatarsal, three weeks in a hard cast, five weeks in an air boot. It was the shit cherry on my already rotten COVID-19 sundae.

Rolling around in a knee scooter was the only way I could get around. I was completely incapacitated. I couldn't even shower unless my husband was there to help me. This was a non-weight-bearing injury, and the orthopedic surgeon was hell-bent on keeping me in a hard cast, but I shamefully resorted to ugly crying and begged the doctor to allow me to have the air boot, promising I wouldn't put any weight on it. The reason was all of the stores were closed, and

Amazon was so overloaded that their usual delivery of one to two days now had become one to two weeks, and I had no wide leg pants to fit over the cast! This way, I could take it off to shower, put on leggings or pajama bottoms, and put it right back on.

But, man, did I look forward to those color-kit-pickup days, a reason to be busy, to get something worthwhile accomplished, get dressed, see people, wear a little makeup, put on a bra. It was like a holiday! My husband would be able to detect that color-kit day was coming. He said I instantly had a happy glow about me, and I was back in work mode. Filling up containers of barrier cream, making labels, setting out the appropriate amount of Tupperware—a new kind of job, but it was the only time during that period that I truly felt like me. We'd make up those kits, and I'd wheel them out to the parking lot in my scooter, which actually came in pretty handy. I could fit four to six bags of color on those handle bars at a time! It felt so great to see our people, see that they were okay, and socially distant catch up like old times.

I knew it was awful for clients to apply their own color, but we were helping them in a moment of weakness. It was an extension of us to them, and they were eternally grateful. They appreciated that we cared enough to supply them with this option, and while they were clueless as to how to execute this task, they made us all proud. Okay, that's a stretch. Many made us proud; many of them, not so much. We make it look really easy, I know, but the joke is that some of these clients are highly educated, extremely smart people…who apparently have two left hands and very little common sense!

One client picked up her color kit on a Thursday. I'm still not sure why, but she opened up the tightly sealed package, poured in the separately wrapped developer, mixed it all together, resealed it again, and waited until Sunday to color her roots. And then she texted me on Monday that the roots didn't cover. No shit! Of course it didn't cover. The color was activated days ago and was now expired!

Someone put theirs in the refrigerator, which serves no purpose at all but made the color rock-hard and difficult to mix, hindering the roots from coloring properly.

Another person assumed the attached container of developer was conditioner even though it was literally sealed to the color container and clearly marked "color activator." Although it was explained thoroughly that you had to pour it into the attached Tupperware of color to activate, they applied raw unactivated color to their roots and took the container of the developer into the shower to use as conditioner after shampooing. Funny but true.

Another client picked up a kit and waited four weeks to use it and contacted me to complain that the color was too dark. Of course it was! It was exposed to the air four weeks ago. It oxidized, and the pigment naturally altered.

I reached out to another client four weeks after she picked up her last color kit to see if she was ready for another. She always came to the salon every four weeks, so it made sense to me that I should include her in that week's pickup. She proudly told me that she still had some color left over from the kit she got four weeks ago. She was storing it underneath her bathroom sink and was planning on using it that next day. OMFG! It's not effective anymore. It's expired! It'll turn her hair black or not work at all! I told her to throw it away immediately!

I tried very hard to explain each detail, and as much as I thought it would be easy for most, I realized we make it look so simple. Aside from giving a full sheet of directions for them to follow, I even recorded a video of me coloring my own hair to show them. Nevertheless, it gave everyone something to do, and even if it wasn't perfect, it was better than roots! And as a true professional, none of these clients' names will ever be released, but as they read this, I know they know who they are!

Everyone was happy to have the option we offered, but there's always one. One client actually complained that the grays didn't cover properly and actually requested a refund. Even at a time when a small business is barely hanging on by a thread, some people are just naturally negative. I refunded her the money she spent, and even though she requested another one weeks later, I refused to make her another kit until we were able to reopen to do it for her instead for fear that it would again be a wasted effort.

Reopening was scary. Georgia and South Carolina were the first states to reopen, so I paid close attention to what the safety protocols would be. It was at that moment that I really thought we would never reopen. The hazmat suits and safety materials they were told to wear and use all day resembled a space suit, with shield, mask, protective clothing draping, and shoe booties. Taking temperature at the door, having clients sign waivers and fully prepay for their services to secure the appointment for them and to avoid the transfer of dirty money.

Each salon can only have one stylist working per day, so not to cross-contaminate and help to remain socially distant. You can only accommodate one client at a time and a mandatory hour between clients to disinfect and sanitize all implements and surfaces with infrared or blue light technology. And it was recommended that you should change your clothes in your car into your work clothes and vice versa so not to bring germs in or out of your workspace. So I'd have to work twelve hours a day and accommodate three clients in a day, a far cry from my usual juggle of ten to fifteen clients a day, and wear a space suit and invest thousands of dollars into air-purification systems and drink Clorox. But try not to cry because you can't remove your mask or shield because it'll contaminate the salon, and you'll have to start all over again.

After hearing all that, I reluctantly told my staff that we will not ever reopen if it had to be like this. A lot of it was overkill. With enough areas reopening before us, many of those rules were softened. We did, however, have to limit the amount of people in the salon at the same time, and everyone needed to wear masks, take temperature, rigorously sanitize every surface and all of our implements, and hope for the best. Luckily, due to my small staff of four stylists, once we were able to reopen, we were capable of organizing a good system for us to work as much as we could and safely still stay within the guidelines of COVID-19 protocols.

But boy, it felt like a full-time job. Many of the clients were confident in our protocols but neurotically anxious the minute someone coughed or came too close. It felt like a game of Frogger, keeping everything clean, moving from one client to the next. Finish the client, move them away from the station to the desk, swab the deck, spray that Lysol, sanitize anything I touched or even looked at, dry it all down, move the new client to your chair, and now clean and sanitize your sink they sat in. Rinse, repeat. All of that with a mask on was exhausting!

That went on for a few months, and just as we started feeling confident that COVID-19 might be behind us, a new strain started up again, and the protocols stayed in effect. And then another strain a few months after that. It was after two years that I decided to allow clients to take their masks off only if they weren't sick or displayed any cold-like symptoms. It did make sense to err on the side of caution. We are hovering two inches from your face. And if hugging wasn't allowed, getting a haircut was one small step from it. But COVID-19 is here to stay, and although no one wants to get it, it is very manageable now.

I will admit, even though I don't miss it, there was some ease of wearing a mask all day. I hardly ever wore lipstick or face makeup, we didn't have to choke on all of the hair spray that we usually breathe in, and I never had to worry if I had a blueberry covering a tooth or salad in my teeth after eating lunch. Just throw that mask back on and move on to the next head!

As you can imagine, there's no way to make money taking care of such a limited amount of people in a day. I was grateful for whatever little PPP money I was able to get from the government. It helped me pay off existing bills and supplement everyone's income to get by. All of my employees came off of unemployment the day we reopened, and we were all so happy to be back to at least this kind of normal. Our hours were long, and we tried our best to safely accommodate as much as we could and still follow the rules.

It was impossible to find new staff to help assist us because no one wanted to come off of unemployment to work. They were getting all of that government assistance and had no desire to stop, so they missed out on an opportunity to get back to work and occupy their day, to grow as part of a great team like we had. It never made sense to me. Was it really worth it to sit around all day scrolling through social media or watching Netflix in lieu of having a job that you could get out and feel like you're getting back to normal?

I would interview tons of people, and once they heard that I am a legitimate business, and I do not pay cash, they ghosted me or outright told that they weren't coming off of unemployment for this job. I do not pay my employees in cash. I named my salon Karma for a reason. Luckily, my entire staff was all paid on the books, so they were able to receive all of the unemployment benefits that were offered. Many cash-pay employees did not qualify for unemployment assistance, so my employees were grateful. And we all know that all good things must come to an end, and we would have to go back to work eventually and stop draining the government of the money they were giving us when we were closed. But true to form, for some of these moochers, months later, when the additional money was discontinued, many of them reached out to me, telling me they were now ready to come back to work. Nope! If you showed your true colors back then, it was good insight as to what kind of employee you would've been now.

The COVID-19 roller coaster. What an exhausting ride—social distance, sanitize everything you touch, vaccine roll out, masks. Just as the coast would look somewhat clear and we thought it was time to lift some of the restrictions, *bam!* It's coming around again! Three years later, and it's still here. We all suffer some form of PTSD from that time, and the way we handle hearing a cough or someone sneeze is forever changed. But life goes on, and we do the best we can…but still with clean, sanitized hands.

Assistants

Oy, where do I begin? First off, I must say that I value the job of an assistant as one of the most important jobs in a salon. They tend to all of the details that go into running a clean and orderly salon. Working a day longer than the rest of the staff, like Jackson Brown said, "They are the first to come and the last to leave." They are the fuel that gasses up the powerful machine of a salon, and without good assistants, we fail. But, Lord, they are hard to come by and harder to keep. Stealing a catchphrase from this new Gen Z population, having to deal with assistants "triggers me."

Before I launch into the horrors of hiring/employing assistants, I will admit that I've had some of the best assistants anyone could ask for during my career. The stylists that work beside me were all my assistants at one time. They grew with me from their start and became full-fledged stylists. We call that *homegrown* in our industry. The seeds were planted at a young age, and they blossomed into beautifully talented creatures that took everything they could from their early years, and I continued to feed their career with whatever education I could offer.

Some former assistants have gone but only left because they decided on a different career path. Some had to be removed because their existence was unprofessional and toxic to our environment. And I think some are in witness protection because they left without a word or valid reason, and I never heard from them again.

We all started as assistants at the beginning of our career. You don't just graduate beauty school and magically start cutting hair behind a chair. You started off the bottom, as how any career should begin. When I started at fifteen years old in 1989, I was the only assistant for a busy salon of five stylists. I spent my days running back and forth like a chicken without a head. Sweeping hair and tidying the mess, making coffee, emptying ashtrays (yes, you could smoke in the salon back then), and shampooing each client all day long by myself. This was back in the dinosaur ages when five to six perms would be done in a day, so I was the lucky candidate to tend to all of those dreaded, stinky perm processes.

I never stopped working from the minute the day began, and I was in constant motion all day long. I used to joke that if I put the broom up my ass, I could sweep while I ran around taking care of everything else. It was grueling work, but looking back, I still believe if I didn't start from that point and do all those menial tasks all by myself, I wouldn't be where I am today. It built great work ethic, and it made me strive to move up the ladder. I loved showing that I could do it, and as exhausting as it was, I was in control, proving to everyone that witnessed that I was a go-getter, and it made people view me as someone special.

Yes, potential assistants, you will have to sweep and mop the floor. You will be responsible for all the laundry. It is up to you to maintain the cleanliness and order in the salon. The days are really long, but if you stay really busy, time will fly. You must be willing to deal with all the personalities and problems that arise in a salon environment. It is required of you to play nicely in the salon sandbox and to get along with all of your coworkers because majority of them have done all of the things that you are now expected to do. It is your duty to shampoo and take good care of our clients, paying close attention to every detail of their care because they are paying your salary. You need to have a positive attitude and work swiftly. And if you play your cards right, the clients will remember your work ethic and happily sit in your chair one day, becoming your client, and refer you to everyone they know *because* they watched you do it all with a smile on your face.

I've always maintained the heart of being an assistant, so I sympathize how hard of a job it can be. I know firsthand the list of responsibilities they have and the grunt work it requires to get done. Tending to the needs of not only the clients but the stylists and staff as well—it's not glamorous, but it teaches you the mechanics of how a business is run, and it's the best first step into this hairy world.

Assistants can be like toddlers. They are new to this field, learning as they go, absorbing every little tidbit of skill and knowledge simply based on what they are seeing and experiencing. I wasn't treated terribly as an assistant, but I did not have it easy. No one showed me how to do it. I was thrown right in to the deep end and had to find my own pace to keep up with the responsibilities. Otherwise, all the wet towels and hair would swallow me up. It sometimes felt like being the tagalong little sister being bossed around by my older siblings. I was working just as hard as the people behind the chairs but with a punch list longer than the day could feel.

And just when you think you're finally part of the team, there's always someone in the tribe who will remind you that you were not there yet. I learned that you have to grow a tough skin to get through that time in your career. It's a hard first step toward paying your dues. The stylists would work all day, demanding 100 percent of my attention, which I worked superhard to accomplish. But when their day was done, they put their scissors away, resprayed their poufy hair, and left for the night, leaving me behind to do my Cinderella duties. Seldom did they offer a hand or say goodbye or express appreciation. And if I griped, I was scolded to stop complaining, reminded that they did this when they first started, that it was a rite of passage, and they paid their dues. I was left behind to finish up the last of the cleaning, tidying, laundry, and mopping to set up for the next day. And man, I hated it. Alone, sometimes I'd cry, which I never did in front of them.

But as hard as it was, I knew I had to earn my place at the table. All alone I stayed, cleaning all the hair spray off the furniture and sweeping away the last of the hair from the floor. The anger and frustration became the fuel I needed to focus on becoming so advanced as a stylist that I would not be an assistant much longer. And that fuel made me what I am today. I promised myself that when I became a stylist with assistants working under me, I would never allow them feel the way I was made to feel. I go out of my way to treat my assistants with respect and remember to be sympathetic to their position.

Even before I owned a salon, I'd lend a hand to help them get their tasks done quicker. I remember back to my nights as an assistant, angrily cleaning up someone else's mess, thinking how unfair it was. Thinking if one of the stylists had stayed to help, how appreciative I would've been.

But the truth is, they weren't being disrespectful. What they did behind that chair basically paid my salary. I was an integral part of the salon, and if I wasn't there to help them as I did, the salon would not survive. I understood that being low man on the totem pole might not be fun, but it's an important role to achieve success. All that hard work groomed me to know every aspect of the beauty industry. Let's face it, any hairdresser would admit if we had to work without the help of assistants, we could not function. We all have our roles to play in a salon, and to me, the assistant is the underdog. They are the reason we can work at the pace we do, helping us accommodate multiple clients at one time, so I respect their position tremendously. They are the extra pair of hands that we need, and they work alongside us to keep our clients happy.

I will not tolerate any employee who bullies the assistants or takes advantage of the fragile newbie status. Even though we have been around longer and might know more than they do, we are all equals in my salon. I've learned we are only as good as the people around us, and the ones who have been around the longest need to lead by example.

But with that being said, assistants are, unfortunately, the ones who give me so much pushback and frustration. They are hard to come by and have been known to be unreliable at times. Lately, I find them to be overly sensitive to rules and authority, and they get overwhelmed very easily, wanting to quit on a dime. If the stylists weren't working as hard as they do behind the chair, there would be no job for the assistants to have. Hairdressers create magic that keeps clients coming back and our bills paid. Although there is no tier system in my salon, assistants have to go through all of the beginning levels and learn as they go to earn their place. It is tough, but if you prove that you are resilient, focused, and reliable, it doesn't take too long.

We as hairdressers have to remember that we walked miles in their shoes. We should take a moment to reflect and always pay it forward, remembering what it was like to be them. I always try to address my assistants with a *please* and a *thank you* and ask, "Can you do me a favor?" when giving them their tasks. I treat them the way I appreciated being treated and also the way I wish I had been when I was an assistant, laying the newfound groundwork for them to follow in that path for the next generation to come.

I think the whole salon industry is suffering from assistant deficit syndrome right now. The climate for this younger generation is baffling and hard for an old goat like me to understand or navigate. I've never seen anxiety like this occur so young in my life. Parents of today coddle their children too much by doing everything for them, making excuses for their behavior, and fixing what ails them by removing all obstacles in their way so they shouldn't trip through life, which inadvertently causes them to have zero work ethic and enables their inability to cope with tasks that are required in a job. The young adults of this generation are made of marshmallow, so soft and affected by the smallest amount of authority. They require soft lighting, a calm voice spoken to them, and a safe space to collect themselves in case they feel triggered by a task, another employee, or a longer than usual workday.

I'm not joking when I tell you that I've had young employees clearly defy job rules, which, in any industry, requires a serious talk, then proceed to lock themselves in my bathroom and cry. And then, I somehow get summoned into a parent-teacher (boss) conference with their parent, who wants to know why their child is getting bullied at work. Bullied? I asked her three times to put her cell phone away to sweep up the hair that we've been tripping over, and then she disappeared to my bathroom for ten minutes to cry.

This younger generation hides behind their parents, and I have to deal with the demands that their parents send them into work to request to me (seriously, this has happened).

- Their precious angel can't work two days in a row. It's too much for them; they need time to relax and regroup.

- Also, Mom and Dad want them home to have dinner with the family, so they have to leave work early—before we are even done.
- They can't work a late night because they need time to come home and study.
- And they can't work *every* Saturday because they need to rest their bodies and deserve to have a social life.

Seriously? Rest? Study? They're on Snapchat and making TikTok videos with all this extra time that they could be putting into work, learning a craft that can teach them as far as they could hope in this world. Their delicate young bones will not break from having to work a few days in a row. Actually, quite the opposite. Let them work hard and build some work ethic. Be proud of them for that. I tell them all, nothing worthwhile comes easy. Luck has nothing to do with it; success comes from hard work—period. Mommy and Daddy are not going to be around forever to wipe your asses and cut up your steak. It's best for them to learn some real-life skills while they are young and fresh.

I've often equated placing ads to hire an employee comparable to being on Match.com. When they answer your ad, you message them in hopes that they'll message you back. Sometimes they do, and sometimes they don't. Not sure why they would apply just to ghost you in return, but it happens more than you'd think. Some respond and are happy to set up a date to interview, but like the hopeful optimist, I prepare to meet my new prospective employee. I clear time in my busy schedule, think of all the things I'd like to say, pick out a professional outfit, remind myself to chew with my mouth closed, like it's our first date. You get the drift?

And like anybody who's been jilted, waiting for that person to show up, they text you a half hour before your meet date about something catastrophic that came up, and they can't meet with you after all. That's actually better than a no-show because I hate to admit that I've waited around with no call, no text, not a word from the person. I'm not sure if it's that they found something more appealing or that people are just not motivated to work these days.

I've placed ads on Indeed and on Facebook job marketplace, and once in a while, I've had some success from those platforms. But I mostly get either uninspired applicants whose mom might've applied for them or some applicants that have absolutely no salon experience. Some applicants haven't worked in a salon in over thirty years, and as much as I appreciate their willingness to work, things have changed in thirty years, so it's comparable to hiring a beginner. During the times of reopening after COVID-19, I experienced applicants who were not willing to come off of unemployment to take the job. They would turn down a perfectly good opportunity to be part of the team just so they did not have to give up the money they were receiving from the government.

I had a twenty-five-year-old girl answer my ad for an assistant position. She was just about to start the ARROJO Academy, a very exclusive beauty school in NYC, and came in early one morning to interview. She was already following our business on Instagram, and when she saw our ad on Indeed, she applied. She was adorable and gushed about our work that she saw from social media and said she knew she would learn so many great things from us. She seemed eager and was ready to jump right in and join our team. It was a busy day, and she was willing to stay that day to start immediate training and learn the ropes. She was superexcited, asking questions about color techniques that we were doing and products that we used. Executing everything she was asked to do with record speed and a smile on her face.

She was there for about five hours until…she asked one of my employees how I paid my staff. She knew the hourly salary I promised from my ad on Indeed, but apparently, she thought this was a cash-pay job. When she heard this was an on-the-books job, that her pay would be in the form of direct deposit, her whole demeanor changed. She asked permission to run out to her car for a minute. She grabbed her pocketbook from the closet and *never came back*.

Till this day, I still think she must've been kidnapped because there was no indication that this eager girl who excitedly took to everything she was doing and seeing would just leave like that. That extra money that the government was paying must've been the dangling carrot to keep her on the fast track to nowhere. So she gave up an opportunity to grow in a fast-paced educational salon for a few extra bucks from unemployment. Or I was right, and she was abducted.

During the COVID-19 lockdown, it was an amazing support to have that extra assistance of unemployment benefits from the government, especially since our doors were shuttered for over three months with no income. But once we were able to reopen, it felt great to return to work, and we rebounded very well. I guess some would rather turn away an opportunity and blow a chance to get back in the game than leave their couch while collecting money from Uncle Sam, watching Netflix, and surfing Instagram reels all day. Tempting, but no thanks. I need a purpose.

The Fine Line Of Employee And Friend

It has been a hard lesson to learn not to get invested in employees personally and learn to draw the line of boss and employee. Through the years, I fell into the pool of employees becoming more like family. We work together in such close proximity to each other every day, and I respect that in spite of what their personal situation might be, they show up and do their job as part of our team. We know how the other person takes their coffee, what they eat for lunch. Hell, we all begin to get our monthly periods on the same cycle; it just becomes that natural. But it could eventually become a little too close for comfort. Not always, but most times, the lines get fuzzy, and both sides can become guilty of overstepping. As a boss, I feel this sense of responsibility to my work family, especially if they are in need. And if I have the means to help them, how could I not? It is risky to cross that line, which occasionally is a lesson that I've had to learn the hard way.

I've had an assistant and her baby live with me temporarily because her home life was unfit for her and her child. Once she got a small apartment for the two of them, I would pick them up every morning. We'd drop her kid off at daycare on our way to work and took her home every night because she didn't have a car. It's not my job to do so, but as a human being, how could I not? Even through her situation, she showed up on time and did her job perfectly, so I felt she deserved it. I feel everyone deserves a chance, especially to experience kindness from a somewhat stranger to help change the direction of the future.

One of my other assistants found herself in a bit of personal trouble and couldn't go to her own family for help, so I had to financially help her out. I understood her situation and knew she deserved a hand. As their "work mom," if they scratch my back, I'll scratch theirs. If they commit to the job and prove they deserve it, I'll swoop in like a superhero to help them out. But don't get me wrong. I've gotten my heart broken dozens of times when these exact people whom I treated like family took advantage of me. But it's my own fault. I overstepped the line and inserted myself into their mess, but at that moment, they needed someone, and I couldn't turn my back on them. They were excellent employees at that time, and I felt it was my responsibility to help them. Fool me once, shame on you, but fool me twice, shame on me. Some people mistake your kindness for weakness, and they grow to expect you to always carry them. It doesn't always work out terribly. Most have never forgotten what I'd done and appreciated the family dynamic we had. But for some, it became abusive, and when I stopped helping, they stopped caring. You live and learn, I guess.

I've mentored certain assistants through the years to come away from the sink and work behind the chair as a full-fledged stylist. I taught them skills and technique and paid for all of their education. I bought them their first pair of scissors and all of the tools they might need. I tried to make them feel important and make their transition from shampoo assistant to a stylist a little easier. It's not an easy road to transition from that job because it takes time to build behind the chair, and you are still expected to help out in the salon when you were not busy working on a client. And because you are not washing hair all day, you are not making as much tip money as you used to make. It worked for the stylists who currently stand beside me and grew with me from the beginning of their career. But not for everyone, I learned. But it doesn't always work out that way. Sometimes they just lose interest or get impatient when it's not happening quickly enough for them, or they take their newfound skill and leave and go somewhere else to practice. Sometimes I feel like the girlfriend who makes a man out of the boy, and they leave to make someone else happy for the rest of their lives. As an owner and someone who is passionate about this business, I want to give whatever I know to someone who wants it. But it burns when you invest and don't get the return. They'll suck up all that you can gave them and find what they think is a better opportunity and move on to greener pastures. Unfortunately, it's the risk you take. It doesn't always end up like that. I work alongside amazing stylists who have been with me from the beginning of their careers. But when it does happen, oh, boy, does it hurt.

I can't change myself, though. I've seen the good it can become. I will always help to grow them and guide them to success. I just need to learn that I can't want it for them. They need to want it for themselves. I know that I just described the definition of *crazy*, doing the same thing over and over and expecting a different result, so I guess call me crazy. For the few whom it worked for, even though the odds were slim, I've witnessed the success.

A few times, I've had the fortunate opportunity to be contacted by some of my former employees. Occasionally, it's to come back to work in our salon again, or it's just a visit and say hi. Sometimes it's sheer coincidence that we run into each other, and we are happy to catch up. Few have used that moment to tell me that it was one of the best jobs they ever had and that I was a great boss. They didn't realize it while working for me, but once they worked elsewhere, they didn't feel the love and support that they had once being employed by me.

One of my assistant-turned stylist did return to our salon after a few years' absence to help us out while I was having health problems. In conversation regarding her return, she admitted that she compared me to a mom figure who was tough and nagged you to do better, to be better, to clean your room, etc., the mom you became rebellious to and didn't quite appreciate at the time. She said it wasn't until she left my salon and I was no longer in her life that she realized how she took me for granted. She recognized how much I tried to support her education and inspire her to grow and flourish, how I folded her into my family and cared for her not only as an employee but personally as well. She didn't receive that from any of the other bosses she went to work for, and it made her realize although I might have been naggy and insisted on perfection from her. I only did it because I believed in her. And then I wasn't so bad after all.

It is my responsibility as the boss to train the assistants. It's my job to help them a form good work ethic and proper skills. Yes, that also means cleaning and maintaining order in the salon because a clean salon is representation of where *you* work. Expect them to be flexible, to be willing to work long days and plenty of them. Trust me, the days will fly right by when you are busy. I inspire them to be mindful and helpful when working alongside the hairdressers. This is an amazing opportunity to learn from them and soak in any creative techniques you watch them do. You have a front-row seat to their talent, like your own personal YouTube channel.

I expect them to take exceptional care of each client and focus on their needs while servicing them. Each client whom you might be washing or draping for color might one day be sitting in your chair. Take pride in your work, show them your work ethic, keep everything tidy, and make clients know that they matter. They will choose you one day for the task when their stylist is out solely based on watching how perceptive and ambitious you were early on. And they will tip you generously because a tip is a gratuity for a job well done. I make sure my staff never views a client with dollar signs in their eyes. I instill in my employees not to expect a tip but to earn it.

I have trained assistants to work with us who have never spent one single hour in a cosmetology program. Some did their sentence of obtaining a thousand NYS (New York State) required cosmetology hours yet didn't feel the need to pursue it any further. You don't have to have an end goal to be a stylist behind the chair to be a salon assistant. It's a good job that you can make great money and work in a safe family-like environment. All I ask is that you take the job seriously, be reliable and fair to the other assistants, and remember that the clients come first.

Some of our past assistants have stayed many years in the position, and the job helped support them as they studied through college. They would eventually move on to their next stage in a different career path. But funny enough, the salon industry is like a cult. Sometimes they reach out and offer to help us out if we are shorthanded. They always miss the smell of aerosol hair spray and reconnecting with our staff and clients.

Assistants—you can't live with them; you can't live without them. If they only knew how important they are.

Oh, the revolving door of assistants. If I ever had any reason to padlock the door and never return to work, it's probably 90 percent about assistant employment.

Most of the time, assistants are young inexperienced newbies, much like unripe green bananas, fresh from the tree, no clue how anything works but eager to find out. Some actually have a bit of experience yet cannot acclimate to the way our salon operates. Some are older with years of salon experience and are at it too long to change how they work, like teaching an old dog newfangled tricks. Some jump from salon to salon, never finding the perfect place, possibly because it doesn't exist, or maybe because they find fault with every environment and will never be happy anywhere.

We try finding able-bodied assistants from the high school BOCES cosmetology programs. We've called the nearby beauty schools, relied on word-of-mouth recommendations, even paid a ton of money putting ads on Indeed and other job-search sites. And it's like finding a needle in a haystack—the good ones are rare. It is a very frustrating venture. Answering applicant resumes is like swiping right on Tinder—starts off as a hopeful booty call, but has no happy ending. Noncommittal applicants—most are unemployed for a reason—they are responsive at first when contacted then wind up ghosting me when it's time to interview. Full of experience on paper, but once tested, they show minimal to no skill whatsoever. And they all had to leave their last salon job due to all of the *drama* they experienced, drama probably caused by them because most drama queens never think it's them.

And even when the stars are aligned and your assistant team is great, a wind blows from the opposite direction, and it turns out that someone is sick, someone is moving, someone is getting a job somewhere else. It's like a game of Russian roulette, you never know each week will bring.

I've said it for years that one day, I was going to write a book on just the craziness I've experienced from salon assistants. Don't get me wrong. As much as I've seen every version of crazy that a salon could see, I've been lucky to have some of the best assistants anyone could ask for. But that's a really small percentage.

Most new employees start out the exact same way—on time, very excited for the opportunity, dressed appropriately, claim to be flexible with our schedule, willing to work as much as possible. Phone is put away without even needing to be told, doing everything that is asked of them.

Fast-forward two weeks later, it all starts to change. Arriving a few minutes tardy to work with a fabulous excuse of traffic or car trouble. All of a sudden, they can't work Wednesday; they have a doctor's appointment. And they need to leave early on Friday; they need to do something with their family. They begin to dress very casually, some resembling bedtime attire. On their phone every chance they get. I know the pattern like the back of my hand. They are a wolf in sheep's clothing. The true colors are starting to shine through. They weren't the right candidate for the job. The good ones excel, absorbing everything they can learn, work with pride and gusto, show up on time, and love being part of the team. They stick out like a diamond in the rough. The others? Just a bunch of lazy cubic zirconias, getting in the way of us doing our job.

Any salon owner can relate. We need good-quality workers to help us do what clients are paying us to do. Assistants are the fuel that keeps the salon going. We need them to survive. But the one thing we *don't* need for survival is deadwood or the problems they bring to the table. I'd rather do it all by myself than deal with some of the issues they bring that I've encountered through my career.

Former assistant employees might read this and know right away that I'm referring to them, like reading a salon version of *The Help*. All names are held, yet the scenarios are 100 percent true.

I invite you to have a laugh at my expense. It is quite comical yet real true-life stories from my experience with certain assistants as a stylist and as an owner. And now you will understand why I drink.

Sleeping beauty

I walk into the back room on a busy day and find my assistant sleeping at the back lunch counter. Not just head down resting with her eyes closed, I mean gently snoring, and she woke up startled when I called her name. The salon was bustling, and the sink was filled with dirty color bowls that needed tending to, so this definitely wasn't the time for a break.

I find out from other employees that she had been caught doing that many times each day the last few times she had worked. Sure, our days can be hectic, and as much as I'd love a little catnap in the middle of the day, when there's a packed salon with a million things to tend to, it's not the best choice to make.

When I explained to her that napping is really not acceptable during work hours, she obnoxiously rolled her eyes and said, "Seriously? It was only for a few minutes."

Run out of excuses

My car broke down. My alarm didn't go off. My dog has to go to the vet. It's my grandma's birthday. My brother's arm fell off, and I have to take him to the hospital. I've heard them all.

I had an assistant who would come up with an elaborate excuse every time she needed off or couldn't make it to work. They were quite creative, I must admit, but relentless, nonetheless. I started writing her excuses down and would catch her reusing the same excuse again! How many grandmothers do you have? And wasn't her birthday last month? She died again?

Tattooed fool

We all have found ourselves in predicaments from time to time. I don't think anyone is exempt from that. Tug at my heart strings, and I fall for it hook, line, and sinker.

One girl found herself in a situation that she was really upset about. She came in on her day off to talk to me, broke down, and explained her issue, asking to take a few days off to take care of this personal matter. She also asked if I could help her out financially because she didn't have the money she needed. This matter was personal, pretty urgent, and was something she couldn't let her family know about.

I never hesitated and went to the bank the next day to withdraw money from my own personal account to give her for whatever she needed. She came to the salon the next day to pick up the money, and I noticed she had a bandage on her neck. Perplexed as to why she had a bandage, I realized why when she began showing the staff the new tattoo she got the day before! I'm paying for your personal issue, but you have money to get a tattoo?

Knowing she was busted, she claimed that she got the tattoo for free, which was highly unlikely. When the chips fall, you need to prioritize your life, and a new tattoo isn't high up on the list of priorities, in my opinion.

When you know, you don't know

It's my job to conference my assistants when they do something wrong. I need to gently explain the problem so they learn the correct way to do it because if they don't, it will perpetuate bad service in our salon. When needed, I would take my young assistant aside and correct him as to proper way to do something, and his reply was always, "I know." When I would tell him that he put a bottle in the wrong cabinet, his reply would be, "I know." When told that he left stains of color on the client's face, his answer was, "I know." I asked him to please get the broom and sweep up piles of hair...you betcha! "I know."

Clearly, you don't know because if you did, you would've done it already, and we wouldn't be having this conversation!

Sick day

It happens. You wake up for work, and you're not feeling well enough to go to come in. My assistant told me just that around 8:30 the morning of a busy day. It's understandable, and as the boss, I now have to scramble at the last minute to try to find coverage to help us get through our busy day. We struggled a bit and had to do some last-minute rearranging of the schedule but somehow got through the day even though we were understaffed.

The next day, the assistant was feeling better and came back to work. I asked how she was feeling, and she told me all about her bad stomach and the horrible migraine headache she had to deal with the day before. She even came in with a prescription bottle of medication to take, so how could I not believe her?

A few hours later, I happened to go on Facebook to post a hair photo for our salon, and I see the assistant was not home in bed nursing a twenty-four-hour virus the day before like she claimed. She spent the whole day goofing around in the city with her friends! She didn't realize one of her friends had tagged her in some pictures, and there was no denying it was from the day before. She wouldn't admit it at first, but she eventually confessed.

I understand that we all need a mental health day, and it's fun to blow off work and have a fun day off. But she chose a day that we were booked solid and knew she was leaving us to suffer without the proper help and did it anyway and then continued the lie into the next day. I've always believed in just being honest, and had I known earlier that she just wanted a day off, I could've made arrangements. And she learned a valuable lesson—social media will always get you in trouble!

Head job

We do not just wash hair at our salon. We provide an enjoyable experience for our clients. Everyone looks forward to a relaxing shampoo, to ease the stress of their everyday life. It makes our job easier if a client is taken care of properly at the sink. They proceed to our chair in the best mood, all of the negativity washed away down our drain. Well, not so much when a certain assistant took care of them. Our clients would emerge from the sink, looking confused, and explain, "That was the oddest shampoo I've ever had!"

There was a strange pressing technique this guy used. He applied intense pressure as he repeatedly dragged his hands from your temples to the top of your head. The look of confusion on the client's face was comical during this experience, but even more hysterical was the look on this assistant's face—eyes closed, face contorted, and concentrating like he was conducting a symphony!

I'd try to get his attention, to tell him to stop and wash the traditional way, but he was completely zoned out during this tantric session. When I asked why he washes hair like this, he claimed that he's trying to heal the client's soul. I told him we don't offer soul healing as a service and that he had to leave.

I found out a year later that he was working at another salon where my friend was a hairdresser. I asked if he still washes hair like that, and my friend said, "He's not allowed to wash my clients. I won't let him make love to my clients' heads!"

Cigarette break

To me, nothing is worse that receiving a service from someone who stinks like cigarettes. We are involved in taking care of clients in such a close proximity. If we smell in any offensive way, it will ruin their experience. I stay away from garlic and onions for that very reason.

During an interview process, a potential assistant asked me three times how many cigarette breaks she is allowed a day. When I explained that we are a busy salon with little chance of leaving the premises to go out to the parking lot for a cigarette, she said she could just stick her head out the front door to take a few drags. Not exactly the image I want hanging right out our front door.

On her first and last day, I allowed her out for one, and she flicked her cigarette butt right outside on the sidewalk in front of my salon door. Bye-bye!

The vulture

We have a standard rule in my salon. The assistants must wait for the stylist to decide who will help them with each client. There is no grabbing at a client to claim ownership or vulturelike behavior to take every client to make the most amount of tips that day. I expedite whose turn it is to assist to keep it fair and equal between all assistants. Some clients will request certain assistants, and we will always oblige. They are paying, and if having that particular person wash their hair is going to make them happy, then I'm happy.

At the end of the day, everyone has had the same amount of people, they all make a nice amount of tips, and no one feels cheated. Sounds easy, right? Not when the vulture is circling. There is nothing I despise more than a hungry vulture among our crew, someone who undermines the rules and tries to steal all of the clients away from the other assistants to make the most tips. I've told everyone who ever worked for me that "the hungriest person at my table is going to be the last person to eat." You can't decide to grab every client who walks in the door. I'm sure everyone learned about sharing back in kindergarten. You need to share with your coworkers and play nicely in the sandbox!

This girl…my blood pressure still goes up when I think of her. A person would walk in, and she would run up to the front and begin leading the person to the sink before we could stop her. She had no idea what service they were getting or which stylist was going to be taking care of them. She was just determined to grab every client on our schedule to leave with big fat pockets of cash each day. She even did this to our mailman one day, not realizing that he's in uniform and only here to deliver our mail! And even when I told her not to, she would sneak over to the other stylists and tell them that it's her turn to help with the next client. And God forbid she was currently washing someone and the next client walked in the door, she'd rush through the client's shampoo to run up and grab them!

And each day, I would pull her aside and school her on her vulture tendencies and reprimand her for breaking our rules. She would gush an apology, tell me how sorry she was, and five minutes later, she was doing it again.

There's just so much of that I was willing to tolerate, so I told her she had to leave. By the next day, she would text me an entire novel full of excuses and emojis, explaining how sorry she was, deflecting that it was everyone else breaking the rules, and begging for her job back. I fell for it once or twice and took her word that she would stop, so I let her back in, but the story always ended the same. So what I learned is if it looks like a vulture and acts like a vulture, it's a fucking vulture.

The fast track to nowhere

I had a young assistant start the path of stepping away from the sink and begin working on clients. She was a talented girl with a tough personality. She was having a hard time completing the NYS cosmetology boards and grew frustrated that she hadn't passed her tests yet. Even still, I saw such promise in her, and my entire staff tried to show her some support. I taught her techniques and bought her new scissors and tools to use for work. I even paid for her to have several one-on-one private haircutting lessons with an educator to advance her skills.

But sometimes the more you do, the more they expect, a lesson I learned that day. She came into work in a foul mood, telling me that she didn't feel appreciated, and she felt I was taking advantage of her. None of us had any idea where that was coming from. We were all so supportive of her process, and with all of the efforts I was putting into her growth, it felt like slap in my face. We decided to shelve this matter till the end of the day when we would have time to discuss it further.

Later that day, without any explanation, she walked out, got in her car, and drove away, leaving us in the lurch. I had no idea where she was going as she headed out the door, and I looked out the salon window and saw her car speed out of our parking lot.

Her two best friends were also our other assistants at the time, and they both asked to speak with me that next day before work, so not understanding this entire situation, I assumed they were probably going to leave as well. Quite the opposite, they already made up a new schedule, happily taking her hours.

I didn't hear a word from the girl after that day until nine years later. She heard I was looking to hire another assistant and reached out to me. She told me that a lot of time had passed and that *she* wasn't mad anymore. Would I consider hiring her back? *She* wasn't mad anymore? I'm so glad *she* wasn't mad. No thanks. I learned my lesson the first time.

Personal hygiene

When you work in a salon, being that we are in the business of appearance enhancement, it is required that you dress appropriately, wear a little makeup, and present yourself in a professional manner. In case you did not know, pajama bottoms are not pants. Dirty flip-flops with unmanicured toes are not acceptable foot attire. A bra or similar undergarment must be worn, especially if your top is sheer and you need one. Personal hygiene is not negotiable.

One would think this would not need to be discussed, but this was the daily issue I had with one former assistant. She would arrive in the morning in a loose tank top (no bra) and droopy old pajama pants. Old flip-flops with chipped toenail polish on two, maybe three toes. No makeup on, hair greasy and up in a sloppy bun, looking like she just rolled out of bed.

One day, she actually asked one of the stylists if she could borrow some deodorant. Into the back room we would go for our daily powwow of how to represent yourself in the beauty industry. She was a sweet girl and a hard worker, and her lack of wardrobe was not an issue of money. It was due to a lack of care. I did not want to hurt her feelings, but it was uncomfortable having her service clients in our salon looking like she was cleaning out the garage.

I laid down the law and told her she wouldn't be able to stay with us if she didn't up her appearance game by dressing up and grooming herself better. But be careful what you wish for. She showed up the next day in a short tight-fitting spandex dress; in five-inch heels; with so much makeup on, she looked like she was going to *The Rocky Horror Picture Show*; and so much perfume on, my eyes couldn't stop tearing all day (which also could've been because I couldn't stop laughing at this situation). Lesson learned: be careful what you wish for.

Fragile bird

We all have issues in our own lives, and we try to deal with it as best as possible. In a salon setting, we take care of so many different walks of lives, and each one will have an individual story or issue. We talk about health, relationships, TV shows, death, recipes, divorces, celebrity gossip, catastrophes—you name it. Clients come to sit in our chair for us to be an ear to listen and to maybe help sort out their personal problems. They do not want to hear about our issues; it is their time, and they are paying us for our full attention.

One assistant would get emotionally distraught whenever she heard the tales of woe from a client's mouth, essentially making it all about herself. She'd excuse herself and lock herself in the bathroom to cry it out, coming out all puffy eyed and sad, effectively ruining her behavior for the rest of the day. If someone's dog was sick, she would cry about her childhood pet. Hearing the story of a client's cancer diagnosis, she would weep about her family member who had cancer ten years ago. Divorce talk? This would set her off about her own divorce that happened years before, causing her to become sad and angry all over again.

I would stifle and divert my client's conversation if I felt it was heading to a sensitive topic just so she could work as needed through the day. There is no way to avoid such conversations in our setting. Clients feel comfortable enough to discuss these personal stories. As a stylist or someone working with the public, it's our job to listen and keep it in their lane. If you can't put on your coat of armor and are going to be affected by the chatter, this is not a forum for you.

Whoudini

Just when you think you couldn't possibly encounter another level of stupidity, one comes walking in the door. Aside from not being able to comprehend simple tasks, like which cabinets the towels go in or where to bring the hair after it gets swept, this one touched the outside of the door of the laundry dryer when asked if the towels were dry yet. How about opening the door of the dryer to see? She must be telepathic because she confidently answered, "No, not yet."

Parent-teacher conference

A sixteen-year-old high school girl applied for the job at the end of the school year. She was the only child to a hardworking single mom, who was thrilled that her daughter would be occupied working all summer while she worked at a doctor's office in Queens. The young girl seemed to take well to the training, showing some hope with her skills. But this was a situation of "when the cat's away, the mice will play."

The mother had no idea that her kid would show up late to work. She left her each morning to walk from their house a half mile away. I would catch her making TikTok videos in our back room during busy work hours, completely ignoring our calls for her to come out and help us. Laundry would go undone, and dirty color bowls piled up in the back sink. She would vape in our bathroom, leaving behind a weird cherrylike smell that, and when questioned, she would swear that she had no idea where it came from. How did I know it was her vape pen? One of my employees drove her home one night, and she took it out and vaped in her car, so she recognized that god-awful scent.

She would stop in the middle of a shampoo to answer her phone or Apple Watch, both of which I eventually took away from her and kept in a small bag in the back room so not to distract her during work hours. She subsequently would steal her phone out of the bag, thinking I wouldn't find out. She began referring to me as her *homegirl* to others and then to my face, which I corrected immediately.

One particular day, she complained about wanting to leave work to go home, and after hours of listening to her whine, I couldn't listen to it anymore and told her to leave. About ten minutes later, my desk manager alerts me that her mom is on the phone, very upset, asking to speak to me. The mom asked me to explain why I kicked her daughter out of my salon. Can you believe this kid? She told her mom that she was getting bullied at work and that I told her to leave.

I had to pull the plug on this and unfortunately tell her mother all that we had to deal with having her child in our work environment. This kid clearly had a problem with authority and had her mother believing that she was this saint of a kid. It's never easy to hear that your child is less than perfect, but I chose not to have kids, so she cannot saddle me with this monster and expect me to deal with this mess on my own while trying to run a business.

So I guess she had to find another employer to annoy because this homegirl ain't having it anymore.

Class clown

Before I opened my salon, I managed the hair department at my former place of work. Being that the owner was never around, it was my responsibility to manage the assistants and train them to work alongside the stylists.

My favorite assistant at that time was also the worst assistant I ever had—always late, always on her phone, walked in first thing every morning asking what time we would be leaving that night, which anyone who has ever worked in a salon knows is never accurate with the last appointment of the day. But, man, was she funny! She could crack me up with her obnoxious facial expressions, her improv jokes, her fake Russian accent when she would mimic our boss, and her dance moves while she was shampooing our clients at the sink.

I know that she knows that I'm talking about her because she is still my friend and client till this day, and she knows I love her, but, OMG, she was awful. She would answer her cell phone while she was washing a client, yelling at whoever on the phone while cradling it with her shoulder. Most days, I kept her cell phone in my work apron, so unless she was going to fight me for it, that's where it stayed all day so not to distract her. Clients used to think I had some kind of sex toy in my pocket because it was buzzing from calls and texts all day long.

She wasn't the best washer either. She left suds in most people's heads and always got their shirts wet but always with an excuse that they moved or lifted their head up when they weren't supposed to. For obvious reasons, she couldn't work with us anymore, but we always kept in touch, and she will still have me cracking up in tears with her Russian accent when she calls.

Thief among us

At my very first salon job, we worked with a girl who unfortunately had a drug problem. Periodically, we would find tip money missing from our drawers and sometimes even our pocketbooks. She even began skimming money out of the cash register, and when we told our boss, he admitted that he knew but never did anything about it. That feeling of violation among coworkers is a huge trigger for me, and the fact that he did nothing to punish her for it made me feel very unsafe. I swore I would never allow myself or my employees to feel that unprotected. But sometimes when the opportunity arises, the nature of people can't be changed.

One of our employees, known to be hugely absent-minded, left her expensive sunglasses in our back room. They sat there for a few days and then disappeared. I figured our forgetful stylist found them and took them back, until she asked me if I had found her sunglasses because she left them in our back room, and now they were missing. I asked some of the staff, and one of my employees told me that she too saw them left on the back shelf but then saw one of our other assistants come in earlier that week wearing them. She questioned that particular employee, saying she believed they belonged to someone else. The other assistant insisted they were hers and acted offended that she would be questioned as if she couldn't afford such a nice luxury. But reality set in, and at that moment, we all knew she was lying.

My manager took her aside and told her the sunglasses were to be returned immediately. I was glad she did the right thing by bringing them back, but once that trust is broken, I can't forgive. I am the mother of this family, and knowing how I felt all those years ago back when my employer didn't protect us, I can't have that under my own roof.

Sacred territory

Everyone loves a great shampoo. Clients look forward to those few minutes at the sink to relax and enjoy a peaceful head massage, letting the shampoo assistant wash all their stress and tension down the drain. Not the case when washed by one chatterbox assistant. She held you hostage with your head in the sink, telling you every detail of her life, rambling on about absolutely nothing, hijacking your few moments of zen.

I would try to catch her attention midway through and gesture to her to be quiet, but she was so involved in her own stories, she couldn't take the hint. Clients would emerge from the sink and complain that she talked the whole entire time, ruining their experience. So oblivious to the social cues, not realizing if the client wasn't responding to her story, that's a clear indication that they do not want to talk.

I would conference her repeatedly to be less talkative at the sink, telling her that the sink is a sacred space and reminding her that clients want a silent, peaceful service. She promised she understood, but instead of following my lead and remaining quiet, she'd begin yammering on to the poor clients she held captive in the sink, laughing that she gets in trouble for talking too much.

Permanent vacation

What my assistants do when they are not at work in my salon is their own business, not mine. Back in the day when I worked as an assistant, I knew damn well that I had to be on the top of my game, well rested and ready to take on the tasks that an assistant is responsible for throughout a busy day. When that day was over, and I had off the next day, it was party till the sun came up. But the night before a workday? Netflix and chill. Or, back in those days, it was Blockbuster video and chill.

I had a great assistant, a mixture of skills and quick wit. All the clients loved her, and she kept the salon laughing with her outrageous personality. But she was a bit of a party girl, who could never seem to get to work on time, or sometimes at all. Always late, usually tired, and hungover, armed with a detailed excuse as to why she was tardy, and a fascinating saga about what occurred the night before. Most of the time I didn't need to hear it, because it was posted in real time on her social media stories, so I'd already know what I had ahead of me before the day even started. After 3 hours of work, and probably 2 hours of sleep she would start to fade, drinking pots of coffee to keep up, essentially dragging her ass and doing subpar work until the end of the day.

We would work a full day together, and the next morning I'd see on social media that she boarded a plane to California to go see a Lakers game or was jetting down to Miami to party her ass off. I'd be a bundle of nerves wondering if she was going to get back on time to work. Sometimes to my surprise, she showed up and got the job done. And sometimes, not at all. The last time this happened I got a text at 4am that she missed her flight home and couldn't make it back to work. Then she went MIA so I was in the dark as to her plans to come back. I knew where she was, because I saw it all over Instagram, but not a word, not a text, nothing. I knew eventually she would show back up, batting her fake eyelashes and apologizing in her sweet little Betty Boop voice, expecting all to be forgiven. But there is just so much a boss could take, and it's impossible to run a salon properly with this type of chaos. I can't invest my energy in someone who is so unreliable, who disregards my business the minute they get an opportunity for fun. I've made a conscious decision *not* to have children, and now I felt I was saddled with one. As much as we all loved her, it was too erratic and not worth the stress to deal with, so I set her free to focus on her partying and good times. Hopefully she can find a way to make it pay her bills.

Front-seat bandit

We get big shipments of supplies on a regular basis, and some orders are bigger than usual. This particular order was huge, and I had my new assistant pack as much of into the trunk of my car as she could. There were a few boxes that wouldn't fit in the trunk, so I told her she could put them on my front seat. I walked out to my car at the end of the day and stood there absolutely flabbergasted as to what I saw. She put the three boxes on the front seat, all right. She put them on the driver's seat *and* left the passenger seat completely empty!

To make matters worse, she wedged those three boxes in so tightly that I seriously could not get them out! How in the world did she expect me to drive home with the cardboard boxes on my driver seat?

Thankfully, I drive a convertible, so at least it gave me an option to take the top down to get those boxes out but not until I had to empty all of the heavy boxes out of the trunk, open the convertible top so I could remove the boxes off the driver seat, and then reload the car again all by myself. Mind you, I just worked ten hours on my feet, and it was eighteen degrees out.

When I called the assistant and asked her why she didn't put them on the empty passenger seat, she said that I never specified which seat to put them on!

Self-taught head case

When I hire an assistant, one of the requirements is to have shampooing experience. It doesn't have to be expert level because we can teach you how we do it, but basic knowledge is expected. Upon interviewing a potential assistant who finished the cosmetology program, she told me she had salon experience and that she knew how to wash hair.

On her first day, I had her wash one of the employees to see what her skills were like. She didn't have a clue. Started shampooing when only half the head was wet down, and her technique was weak. After rinsing, she left suds all throughout the head and couldn't figure out how to brush the hair out.

Baffled how a person who had salon/shampoo experience could do such an awful job, knowing I couldn't have her wash our clients with such subpar skills, I had to have a meeting with her to figure out the problem. And I did.

- She had *gotten* her hair done in a salon, so that's why she *had* salon experience (please don't laugh…I know).
- She washed several mannequin heads in cosmetology… and she washes her own hair.

I guess that qualifies, right?

Believe it or not, these are only a few of the laughable experiences I've had in my journey as a salon owner. As I have said, you seriously can't make this shit up. And you wonder why I drink?

How To Be A Successful Stylist 101

You want to be busy? Then get busy. Learn something new every day. Use the tools of social media by showcasing your work to promote yourself. Give out your business cards. Tell your clients that you would love if they referred their friends and family. Clients don't always come to find you. You have to put yourself out there and reel them in.

And sometimes, that means you will have to work a little bit more. Be flexible and willing to work extended hours to accommodate as many people as you can, especially in the beginning of your career. Your scissors don't start working at 10:00 a.m. and automatically stop at 6:00 p.m. Come in a little early to take care of that grateful client. Stay late to fit in that appreciative customer; she/he will never forget it. Our industry is built on accommodation, and it speaks volumes if you are flexible like that. Remember, if you turn your back on them, there's a million other places they can go.

However, there are times that you are so accommodating that certain clients will take advantage. If you fit them in once at the last minute, they seem to think they don't have to schedule an appointment ahead of time anymore in the future. There's a fine line to being accommodating and being a doormat. What clients need to recognize is that although we perform our tasks so elegantly and make it seem to happen like magic, it is still an art and should be valued as such. It might look easy, but the brainpower, physical strength, and creativity that goes into every move we make is an exhausting feat. And somehow, we do get it done. But to throw in one more ball to juggle is tough, and it will compromise the integrity of our work. So be open to accommodating your clients and know why or whom you are doing it for. Loyal clients will appreciate your extension of time, but beware of those who might abuse their privileges. It's okay to say no and teach them to have no other option but to book ahead like everyone else if you realize their last-minute habit is becoming chronic behavior.

One of our clients always prebooks a few of her next services. Her husband is a call-today-for-ASAP kind of guy. The wife has literally begged us to punish him by *not* giving him an appointment if he called last minute. She has worked hard all of these years to train him to respect appointments and said if we accommodate him immediately, it's ruining all of her hard work!

You should always dress for success or at least dress professionally in a way that your clients will be inspired and proud to have you as their person. I've always been an overdresser. Even in my early years as a shampoo assistant, I took pride in what I wore and how I coordinated my daily ensemble. And clients began to gravitate to me, take me seriously, and trust that if I could showcase myself in that way, I'm sure to do the same for them. A motto I learned early on: "Always dressed, always ready, always busy." And it doesn't mean you need a million-dollar wardrobe; just make sure your hair and makeup are done and you are dressed presentably. As previously mentioned, most times, my hair stays in that wet bun from my morning shower, but it looks clean and deliberate, so it constitutes a polished style.

Looking good builds your confidence and boosts your self-esteem, and when people compliment you, you know you've made your mark. It feels good to dress nicely, and there's a sense of power that comes along with it, especially when you work in the beauty industry. No one wants to sit in the chair of the stylist who looks like they just rolled out of bed. How can a client take you seriously or trust your skills if you do not look the part? I believe that it's up to the boss to lead by example and have an image that these young budding stylists should follow.

One of my mentors, Geno Stamporo, had said, "Dress up to the money you want to make." That statement has stuck with me from the moment I heard it. Do you want to make a ton of money, have people trust you and take you seriously? Then throw on those heels, do your hair and makeup, and even if you have to, borrow clothes from your parent or sibling's closet to dress the part. You'll be so impressive, become so busy behind the chair, and be in such high demand that you will have to turn people away. Clients will be proud to sit in your chair and will be proud to refer you to others.

You want to squeak by, making the bare minimum, putting in the bare minimum, looking like the bare minimum, being half booked all the time? Then all you will receive is the bare minimum. By all means, roll out of bed, wear your pajamas to work, and throw that dirty hair in a ponytail. You can kiss those referrals goodbye. Clients would be embarrassed to refer you in that state or would not trust that you can make anyone look good, especially if you can't even do that for yourself. It's all about image. Represent yourself in the beauty industry. We are their glam squad, and they want to follow our lead. And trust me, you'll be counting the cars that drive by all day while you sit around the salon looking sloppy, doing nothing. The message is if you want it, then look it.

Inspire your clientele by always staying ahead of new styles and trends. Regardless of how long you have worked behind the chair, you can always learn something new to bring to your clients. It can be a new color trend or a new dry shampoo spray. Clients come in thirsty for something new. Styles change from year to year—actually, season to season. Be creative and prepared to shift the same style into something that works for that time. It's summer; let's add a few brighter highlights around the front crown to make your hair look sun-kissed. Winter is coming; glaze those existing highlights with a rich, deeper tone to shift the color into something appropriate for the colder months. It doesn't have to be extreme, just a moderate twist of something close to what they already have. Learn about new products or techniques; let them leave each time with another helpful tip or product to execute their style.

The way to lose clients is to become stale. Don't be that stylist who thinks they've learned everything they will ever need to know. If that is the case, pack up your scissors and put yourself out to pasture because your time behind the chair is done. I worked with a stylist who had that kind of mindset, never wanting to grow or partake in any of our educational classes or workshops. She had a stubborn know-it-all attitude. She clearly needed the education to stay relevant but outright refused. Her work was so antiquated; she actually still referred to highlights as a frosting! She had the least amount of clients each day, and most of them looked like they had the same dated style from twenty years ago. I guess some of her clients were okay with that, but most were completely blown away once they had someone else service their hair and bring them back to life. They were offered ideas and options and had their hair finally look up to date, and that's when they saw the difference, and they never looked back.

As their chosen glam director, clients look to us for proper guidance for their look. It is based on the trust and confidence they have in our work, and it is an important part of our existence in their lives. We need to stay current. It keeps us relevant, and it keeps them coming back for more.

Another important lesson is to learn to be consistent. Remember the lines of their previous haircut and log in any changes to their color records. When a client loves what you do and requests it again, it's imperative that we duplicate it as best as possible. Remember that they like their bangs long or that they have wicked cowlicks to not make certain areas too short. They put their faith and trust into our work and expect consistency. No one likes to expect perfection and walk away with a different variation of what they had. The best compliment a client can pay you is to request the same as they had on the last visit. Like getting the same dish again in a restaurant, asking for a repeat performance is a testament to their happiness in our work. Some do not like to change but value the ease of coming to us for our consistency.

Stylists need to change up their own hairstyle as well. I am laughing as I write this because I have a tendency to make the least amount of changes to my look because I'm too busy running a business to keep it up. I do my part to look polished and professional at all times, but those highlights would be grown out for four months before I have a chance to retouch them. And the last few times I've had my hair colored, it was by yours truly, in my own bathroom at home after work. One day, I aspire to practice what I preach, but as long as it's done and fresh and can inspire the clients, it counts. All stylists should change up their cut from time to time, alter their color, throw in a few extensions for thickness and/or length to give clients an idea of something new to do. Be a walking advertisement for the next best thing, showing clients quickly modified changes that can be made to make it look new.

Promote professional product use and give your client a dissertation on the *who*, *what*, *when*, *where*, and *why* of product use and proper hairstyling. What are their hair issues? How are they styling their hair? When and where are they applying product? How much are they using? Become the professor of hair knowledge and troubleshoot your way into their solution. When they see your passion for the welfare of their hair, alongside your professional understanding of each product, they will be forever grateful and follow your lead.

Know all of the retail products your salon carries and sells and, as a good team player, recommend those products to your clients to use as home care. I have always taken advice from my stylists as to the products they feel comfortable using and have stocked our shelves with what they like. As trained professionals, we are educated to know what would work best in each situation and have high-quality items readily available for them to purchase to take home. Try not to recommend outside products for clients to seek out themselves; the business of retail sales should stay in-house.

Stand out among other stylists and show genuine care and concern for their look. Clients are a reflection of you, and when they sit in our chair, we become the bus driver, driving them safely from point A to point B. When they feel like a million dollars leaving the salon after their visit, it's your words that will resonate in their heads. Your tips and recommendations will become reality to them, and from that moment on, they become lifelong clients. It's up to you to guide them and educate them so as a walking billboard, they represent you out in the world.

I might not know everything there is to know about the hair industry, but one thing I do know is client retention. I have clients who have been with me for over thirty years, and they still feel inspired by my work because I never stop learning to offer them new ideas. No one keeps the same style for all of that time, and I've worked overtime to keep myself relevant in their eyes, to keep them looking current with each year's changing styles. I give them no reason to leave me because I stay ahead of the curve to keep their hair looking current. They all know that I always have their best interest in my vision.

That is why stylists lose clients. They don't know everything there is to know behind the chair and begin to grow comfortable, thinking clients will not leave them. If you don't constantly educate yourself to bring something new to their table, they will find another table to sit at. We don't own clients; they make a conscious decision to sit in our chair. Whether it is their first visit, or their hundredth, treat them with the same respect and bring it. Give them every reason to stay with you and every reason not to leave. It is a full-time job staying on the top of the heap, so if you want it for the long haul, follow my lead.

Desk Duty

The reception desk is the first experience in a salon. It's the place where most clients will make their first impression. When they walk in, are they greeted immediately, or do they stand there and wait for someone to acknowledge them? Did the receptionist smile and have a pleasant attitude? When they call to make an appointment, are they kept on hold or spoken to in an abrupt manner? If they are not able to get the time slot that they want, are they offered to be put on the cancellation list for any future openings that might work for their desired time? Upon checkout, were they asked to rebook their next appointment and given it a proper goodbye? It might seem simple, but unfortunately, in many salons, this is where you lose the customer.

The desk is the heartbeat of the salon. Appointments are finalized, money is exchanged, phone calls are answered, and plans are made. A salon is like the ocean. For a moment, it's calm; the salon is clean and orderly, no phones are ringing, just the gentle hum of a blow-dryer. Five minutes later, the tide rolls in, and there are four people waiting to get shampooed, three people lined up to check in or out at the desk, both phone lines ringing, the UPS guy is wheeling in eleven boxes of supplies, and hair is piling up to our ankles.

So the desk manager is like our lifeguard, responsible for our function and order, rescuing us when we are drowning. They are always ready for the floodgates to open, in charge of keeping things running like a well-oiled machine. Seeing problems before they happen and smoothing out issues until there aren't any. Swiftly expediting tasks in order of importance. Understanding every product we sell, so they can better educate the clients when the stylists are too busy. Multitasking by maintaining communication between clients, operators, and assistants. And all the while, in charge of every appointment made and every dollar in and out of our register. It's no easy task. I feel it's probably the most mentally exhausting job in the salon, and they never even touch a single strand of hair!

I've always believed that when a client enters through our door, the clock begins, and their experience has begun. Nothing irks me more than a busy desk receptionist completely unaware of a person standing in front of them, waiting to be seen. All it takes is eye contact, a pleasant smile, and a quick gesture to show that although they are currently busy, they notice the client and will be with them in a minute.

After checking them in, the desk alerts the operator that the client has arrived and judges if they are ready to begin their service. It is not unheard of for a stylist to run a few minutes late, so when that happens, I expect my manager to pay attention to the time and call to alert the client not to rush. Nothing worse for a client who rushed to be on time for their appointment to walk in and see their stylist running late, especially when they could've taken their time, stopped for gas, ran home to let the dog out, or even run an errand. It's even worse for the operator, having your client angrily stare at you from the couch, annoyed that they rushed for nothing, thus already ruining today's experience.

At reception, it is important to keep all necessary information on each client regarding service history, contact info, recent purchases, and help figure out when they will be due back for their next service. Desk managers maintain the stylist schedule and properly adjust appointments to keep an even flow throughout the workday. And at the end of the day, they become an accountant, tallying credit card transactions and service tickets and adding up the till from the day. And then they go home to a quiet room and drink in silence.

The new trend in the salon world is a contactless virtual desk. No one to check you in as you arrive. No receptionist to take your payment because you pay for your services via Venmo, Apple Pay, or any other technological way of online pay. No calling on the phone to schedule your appointments; you message the stylist or use salon software to set them up yourself.

Although I know this is the way of the future, it is losing the personal touch salons have always been known for—a person designated at the front desk to greet you when you walk in the door or to give you a farewell goodbye as you leave. The conversation that takes place regarding that special occasion you need that appointment for. The person you talk to on the phone when you discuss the tough reason why you need to reschedule your appointment. Last-minute recommendations as to hair products to take home to use. Any of my desk managers will agree that they have built friendships with our clients throughout the years. They have bonded over beauty needs and gray hair, traded recipes, and conversed about holiday gatherings and family nonsense.

My desk managers have smoothed out potential issues by having simple casual conversation due to the personal connections they have made with each individual client, whether it be over the phone or in person. Imagine a client is about to leave the salon not 100 percent satisfied with her service. The desk manager can pick up on that vibe while at checkout and, through conversation, will find out what is wrong. If the client thinks, for instance, that the color is a little too light or that the bangs are still too long, the desk manager is able to communicate that to the hairdresser in record time.

Now imagine that client, without a receptionist being able to buffer that issue, going home and becoming more unhappy by the minute. As it festers, the minor issue begins to build up, and the client resorts to texting the stylist an escalated version of their unhappiness. Human connection puts people at ease, not left alone to their own devices. The desk manager is groomed to understand the body language and level of happiness of each client as they are leaving. They can put that client's mind at ease and show just by being observant that they care if an issue does arise and proactively keep the stylist updated as to what they have observed because stylists move on to the next client right away and might not have the ability to gauge a client's issue.

I, for one, try never to go to the self-checkout aisle when I'm in the store because I prefer to have a cashier ring me up simply because there's usually a question, light conversation, and personal contact that I feel is necessary when going through minor transactions like that in life. And there's a big chance I won't be able to probably remove the theft detector off the item, so they will inevitably have to come to my rescue anyway!

These days, with all of this technology, we are forgetting how important human contact is. Since COVID-19, so many people have expressed the joy they feel to be in a social environment such as ours, especially since many are now working from home and having all their things delivered instead of venturing out in public. It feels like a sense of normalcy to be with other people, having face-to-face conversations while receiving services done by an actual human. Thankfully, hairdressing skills are not obsolete or replaced with AI technology, or at least not yet! Most of what we have always done behind the chair requires the skill of a person's hands and the authentic creativeness of their brain. It can never be replaced by punching a style into a computer, like Judy Jetson does in the famous cartoon *The Jetsons!*

Most of the desk managers who have worked for me were clients of mine before I hired them. They experienced life in our salon as a client and were happy to join our staff when an opening occurred. Although it is a tough job with many stressful moments, they work at a fun, sociable environment, where they observe people coming in sad and leaving happy. Now, as a staff member, they became the other end of that exchange. They are able to experience the magical transformation of a client, being the first *and* the last person that client sees. They've built many strong relationships with each client and become part of their salon journey. They speak to the clients on the phone and greet them hello and goodbye each time they come. Now experiencing both sides of the field, they understand how much goes into one individual client, knowing how it feels to have been a one-time recipient.

One of our early desk receptionists was actually a client of mine from the time she was eleven years old. A few years later, around the time I opened our salon, Ashlee was a budding freelance makeup artist whom we would hire when makeup was needed for weddings, proms, or special occasions. I asked Ashlee to help me out in our salon in a pinch when our salon manager left, and she offered to work at our desk until I hired someone with experience to replace her. Having no desk experience at all, she learned as she went. She had amazing people skills being a makeup artist, had the most positive attitude, and brought such joy to our desk, it was almost infectious. Everyone loved walking in to see her, and she had a unique way of diffusing tension if it ever occurred. It was through her experience that I realized how important it was for the front desk to be so uplifting. It instantly made people feel great the minute they walked in the door.

The only downside to Ashlee, bless her heart, was that she was terrible when it came to math-related money transactions. She was the most positive employee I ever had at my desk, but she got so caught up gabbing with clients that they sometimes left without making their next appointment or paying their bill! At the end of each night, we would both spend hours redoing the register, going through each ticket and every receipt. So upset with herself, she would apologize each time, admitting, "I'm not good at math. I'm only good at making people pretty!"

As stressful as it might've been, I didn't mind much at all. The previous desk manager was the polar opposite of Ashlee, always in a bad mood with a curt attitude. She did a good job, but it grew difficult to deal with that kind of negativity on a daily basis. Her demeanor was ruining the culture of the salon, and as much as I tried to fix it, it was an impossible task. The clients felt it, my other staff members felt it, and it wasn't great for business. Experiencing Ashlee's positive demeanor made me see the light. I'd rather spend all night counting transactions, fixing appointments, and figuring out mistakes in the register with Happy Ashlee than spend another day with Miserable Maude.

I don't think I will change my mind and adapt to this new concept of a deskless salon. I firmly believe, especially coming out of previous COVID-19 isolation, most individuals crave the closeness of people and need some familiar human contact to feel comfortable in a salon setting. I've built a career on clients gravitating to our small salon setting, expressing how grateful they are for our family-like community. Call me Wilma Flintstone, but this is an aspect of our industry that I will probably not budge on. I can't allow our salon culture to adjust to technology rather than the environment our clients love. I'm sure it would benefit me from a business point of view by helping my bookkeeping become easier and can ease up the pressures of the desk duties. But human contact is so needed these days and is what I feel is lacking in our society right now.

And I don't have to assimilate. It's my business, and the last time I looked, I made the rules. As my mother told me back when I was a kid, "When you grow up and have your own house, you could make your own rules." Thank you, Mom. I think I will.

Clients

If your hair looks good, it's like you can conquer the world. A perfect hair day should come with a soundtrack. All day long, you hear Lizzo singing "Good as Hell," the birds are chirping, and the sun is shining. There is no traffic on the road, and you even snag a prime parking spot right in front of where you are going. All is good in the world.

But if your hair looks like crap, now that's a different soundtrack. Imagine that creepy melody from the movie *Sleeping with the Enemy* is on constant replay, and thunder and lightning are booming in the background on a cold, dreary day. Your lunch tastes stale, your coffee is cold, your car has a flat tire, and you know for sure you are going to run into an old boyfriend or the girl you hated in high school looking as hideous as you think you do. We've all been there. The visual is true.

What is most challenging for a hairdresser is that we are relied upon to turn everyone's day right side up, to keep them as beautiful as they've grown accustomed to and turn that frown upside down. We have the power to change their attitude, lift their mood, and turn them into someone new. A good hair day can change the course of one's day. We have to be creative by nature, have the innate ability to decipher their vision, and somehow deliver…all with a smile on our face. It's no easy task, but it's somehow our job to make it look easy.

Eric Fisher, a mentor from Aquage, once said, "Hairdressers are like ducks. Clients see us effortlessly gliding on a lake. What clients *do not* see is that under the water, our feet are paddling like hell, working like mad to stay afloat, to get from one point to another."

It's our job to stay calm and appear calm to keep you calm. We are the flight attendants of the salon. The oxygen masks are dropping from above, yet we are walking around with the drink cart, acting like nothing is wrong. We could be in the middle of a dilemma with your hair, but if you see us panic, you will panic, so we don't. We have to maintain composure and make it seem like everything is totally fine…even if we are running a half hour late and don't have enough time to execute this miracle that you expect us to create.

Listen, it's just hair. We are not brain surgeons. In the world of all the problems we have, hair is not the biggest dilemma. But looking good is the one thing that can shield you from your other problems, and when you look good, it makes life easier to function. As insignificant as it might seem to others, you can't put a price on a good experience that makes you look pretty.

Clients make a conscious decision to have us take care of their beauty needs, and they are the reason we get up in the morning. If it wasn't for them, we'd be lounging around the salon all day long with nothing to do. The staff would all have perfectly coiffed hair because if you aren't doing your job properly, clients don't come in, leaving you with all of that extra time to primp yourselves.

I was taught to take pride in the fact that although there are a hundred options of other salons from your clients' front door to yours, they are choosing you to do the job. Whether it's their first appointment or their hundredth, you should treat them exactly the same so they feel confident that they made the right decision in staying with you. We are not only in charge of their hair in that moment, clients rely on us to guide them through new looks and to inspire new ideas for the changing times. We are also their therapist, sort of like their own personal bartender, because they feel so relaxed in our chair that they feel comfortable enough to let us into the nitty-gritty of their lives, telling us where all of the bodies are buried.

One of the problems we as hairstylists face in our industry is that we have become superheroes in our clients' eyes, like modern-day magicians. They come in with a few pictures, and we are expected to create like we have a magic wand or a unicorn in the back room that will make all of their dreams a reality. And knowing that they view us in that light, it has pumped our ego so much that we actually begin to believe that we can.

Until we can't. That's when the truth comes out. We are not the great Wizard of Oz. We are just a bunch of regular Joes, pushing the buttons behind the curtain. Once they figure out that we are all just mere mortals like everyone else, they might leave us to find the *real* wizard, the next hairdresser who can perform such magic.

Sadly, clients need to realize that we are just people, and we are trying the best that we can. We are beauticians, not magicians. We appreciate that you hold us in such high regard, but you need to understand that the relationship between a hairdresser and a client is a partnership. Go into your services with a goal, but more importantly, an open mind and realistic expectations. And recognize that sometimes, your goals are more of a journey, so it might take a few visits to get you there, but if you are patient, we can do this together.

If you trust your hairdresser and they tell you that your goal or idea is not a good one, it is your job as a client to listen to them. Period. End of story. I have learned early on from failed client experiences that as the professional, you need to be the captain of the ship and refuse to do work that you know will not look good or benefit the client, especially if it is a style that the client in question does not have the skill or the ability to achieve on their own or will possibly compromise the health of their hair. Stylists must stand firm when it comes to unrealistic goals that will inevitably harm the hair and cause heartache to both the client and the stylist. Some hairdressers just do not have what it takes to tell their clients no for fear of hurting their feelings or seeming incompetent as an operator. In the end, all we want is what's best for our clients...and for our reputation.

But we hear it every day. "Kim Kardashian went from dark brown to platinum blonde in one day." Good luck with that. Her hairdresser is no magician. He just knows how to hide the damage to make it look good. What most don't realize is if they saw Kim Kardashian's hair up close, they would see that her head is filled with hair extensions, and it is so processed, it probably looks as dry as the hair on a troll doll. It's trick photography that makes it look great, that and a hairdresser who follows you around every day to try to keep it looking healthy. Unrealistic expectations are common in the salon chair. Everyone believes whatever they see on social media, so they turn to us as if we are hair wizards. But the truth is it is not always that easy. Your point A to point B will most definitely have a few detours to get you to your final destination, if the destination even is obtainable.

I've been referred to as the Nazi hairdresser many times in my career. I run a very tight ship, and to retain my business this long at this success rate, I've proven that being the "bad cop" works. I say *no* very easily and not because I like to be mean. I'm just not going to give false hope when I can clearly predict a negative outcome. If I don't feel good about it, I am not going to do it. I cannot compromise someone's hair just because they want to look like the person in the picture when I know their hair will not be able to achieve that result. Most people who refuse to listen, who go elsewhere to achieve their goal, will usually wind up back in our chair, tail between their legs, whispering those magical words that I must admit, I love to hear: "You were right. I went somewhere else and did it anyway. Help me! Look what happened to my hair!"

The only good thing that comes from this type of experience is this newfound level of trust that a client has for your work and business practice and will listen to you the next time they come up with a not-so-brilliant idea. The lesson they've learned is that as their hair guru, it is our job to be their protector and to always have their hairs best interest at heart. All good hairdressers have to follow that rule. It's gospel. If you value your clients, and your gut is telling you that it's wrong, don't do it.

Many times, my refusal to deliver a style or a complex color change is because the client will not or does not know how to handle it at home. Not everyone is skilled with a blow-dryer or has the desire to put in the work, and most styles require effort, proper products, and time. If I know my client, and I know that she has two left hands and will not participate in the effort that style will require to handle it at home, I gently decline and deter. Some styles require a commitment to come back to the salon frequently to maintain, and if I know the client has a habit of waiting months between appointments, it's not worth trying. It could be the best haircut or the most fabulous color, but if they cannot style it at home or commit to the frequency it will need to maintain, it's a horrible idea.

Oftentimes, I have created a new look on someone, and I run into them in public, and I try hard to hold back my despair. It looks like their old style because they are still styling it the old way! Or the color is all faded and oxidized because they didn't follow directions as to the proper care at home to keep their color fresh. And because of their love and loyalty to you, they are walking around, telling everyone that you did it. That's a terrible walking billboard showcasing your work, inadvertently ruining your reputation. And that is no way to pay the bills.

It is imperative that by the time a client leaves your chair, you have explained all the things they will need to duplicate your work at home.—tips on how to style, recommended products to achieve a good result, what *not* to do in order to make it look it's best. Remember, your reputation is 50 percent what you do in your chair, and it's 50 percent what they do at home. Teach them what they need to know before you find yourself having to look for a new career.

Hair Therapy

Hair is emotional. It's a way to express your feelings, to take some risks to make changes to the course of your life. It's your crowning glory, and it's often the first thing we see on a person, which makes it so important in our eyes. Sometimes it's a comfort, and when you find you are not at your best, it is smart to leave it alone and revel in the consistency of it.

Way too often, people make bad decisions for their hair based on emotion. A break up, a few pounds overweight, stress from their job, boredom—you name it. I just broke up with my boyfriend; let's cut bangs. I hate my job; let's do a radical new color. I look fat, and nothing fits; let's hack it all off. I will spend my entire career wondering why we all take it out on the one thing we love so much.

That being said, I must add myself to the equation. Guilty as charged. I should know better, but I'm just like the rest of you. I've given myself bad-day bangs many times in my life, like cutting a fringe would miraculously make everything better. *Wrong!* Now I can add to the pile of misery "hating my new bangs," which, coincidentally, never seem to grow out quick enough when you want them to.

There are times where your hair is greatly affected by the different phases your body goes through. It has been said that a person's body goes through a hormonal change approximately every seven years. In addition to that, we all experience hormonal changes after stressful occurrences, pregnancy, surgery, medicine, and as we go through traumatic phases in our lives.

Prepubescent kids begin to experience greasy, frizzy, hard-to-manage hair as their skin begins to secrete an overabundance of oil. Parents already have to deal with their squeaky voices, stinky body odor, and wild teenage mood swings, so they rely on us to school their mutant teenagers on the proper way to wash and handle this problem.

New mothers will most likely experience a temporary bout of excessive hair shedding after having a baby due to their hormones readjusting back to a normal state. Nothing scares me more than the raging hormones of a pregnant woman. Even worse is a postpartum mom who is cleaning clumps of hair out of the drain after taking a shower.

Hair loss can also occur after having COVID-19. Within three months after the virus leaves your system, many people experience radical hair loss. Some are shedding right from the scalp, and others experience some midstrand breakage, leaving your hair to feel weak and much thinner. It will eventually stop, and with time and good products, it can correct itself, but seeing all that hair in the drain can be extremely traumatizing. Pair that with the risk of blood clots, respiratory issues, and brain fog, this virus is the gift that keeps on giving! The technical term for this type of hair loss is called Telogen Effluvium—or as we call it, "COVID-19 hair." Hair shedding can occur after experiencing a high fever or a virus. I have found that many of my clients experienced this type of hair loss after dealing with COVID-19, so it makes sense that it's a long COVID-19 symptom. So much research has been done about this, and every day, we are learning what can be done to help avoid it, to help strengthen and repair your hair to get you through this emotional time.

After a surgical procedure or medical treatment, your hair will seem lackluster and begin to grow in differently. Anesthesia and medicine will invade your new regrowth as it begins to leave your body.

As we approach middle age, it seems although our waistlines are increasing, our hairline is shrinking! Hair loss is possible, but in most cases, our strands are just getting thinner. In reality, our hair follicles begin to decrease in diameter, resulting in a thinner, more sparse appearance.

In our older phases of life, our scalp does not produce as much oil as it once did, so our hair loses shine and elasticity. Hair loses its youthful glow and can either become weak, showing a loss of body, or becomes very coarse and wiry due to the lack of natural lubrication our scalps once provided.

During these changes, this is when a stylist becomes not only a therapist but a lab coat biochemist. Clipboard in hand, we have to recite a dissertation on the affects that hormones have on our hair. As their chosen stylist, we need to hold the hand of each panicked person who sits in our chair, reassure them that all of this is normal, yet find them an effective solution to help their hair dilemma and their sanity.

One thing we are taught *never* to do is to first blame hormones for the reason a client's hair is not handling well. We might know damn well that it is the culprit, but it is unprofessional to deflect and just assume that it has nothing to do with our work. And if they are in fact hormonal, that's a damn good way to get slapped by a raging client! Instead of just blaming hormones, dig deep and see if maybe your usual approach might not be working for them anymore. Hair becomes fragile over time, and we might need to make adjustments on how we process their hair, the products that we use, or the amount of heat exposure they are now capable of handling. If we jump right in and blame good old Mother Nature, that reads to a client that we are not taking any responsibility for our actions that could be contributing to their situation.

I'm grateful to have clients who have been with me for so many years, and I've seen many of them through several of these tough hormonal phases. From childhood, to puberty, through pregnancy into menopause, and then some, these difficult times can be very challenging, and this is when our job consists of more than just scissors and hair spray. These changes are extremely emotional, and we are a source of comfort and a helping hand to guide our people through the darkest of times because everyone has some sort of issue, and looking good is a shield to help get you through it.

There are times when clients hare present in my salon but are emotionally somewhere else. Regardless if they just received bad news about a death or got a bad health diagnosis, even trouble with their kids, it happens every day. One client even found out her husband was cheating on her while sitting in my chair, getting her hair colored. And they either choose to freak out and tell us right away, or they sit there quietly, saying nothing and marinating in the unhappy news. It's our job to pick up on their distraction, understand it is coming from a place we just don't know about, and act accordingly. So I continue in silence so not to distract them, or I become the comedian who has to keep them distracted, laughing, and occupied so they can have a semipleasant experience while they rationalize what their next steps will be.

Whatever they need—this is where the hairdresser-client relationship goes beyond the boundaries of just business. We become family to them, and we have to be very in tune to the moods and their body language and understand that this appointment is a pleasant distraction from what could be causing them pain. If they want to tell us, they will. And if they choose not to, we just make their experience pleasant until they can take care of what they need.

One of my clients left her mother's bedside at hospice because she needed a break and came to get a manicure. She didn't know where to go and said this was the only place she could disconnect and feel like she was with family yet didn't have to talk. We were all aware of her mom's situation, so there was no need to discuss. She needed a change of scenery and to be around people who would silently comfort her as a welcome distraction. When someone is going through such a difficult time, they need to give themselves a break to regroup and reassess to then go back to the inevitable. It's part of our mission—to give great services in a comfortable family-like setting and make our clients feel welcome, make our setting so special that they can treasure it as a welcome escape even if it's only for a half hour service. No one knows the struggles people go through, but for them to choose to come to us, whether they tell us about it or not, is when you know you've achieved something special.

Having clients as long as I've had, these connections go far beyond the chair and the scissors. We are intertwined in each other's lives…good, bad, or indifferent. Like a marriage, we are there for better or for worse. Whether it's doing the bride's hair for her wedding or unfortunately shaving a client's hair after they start chemotherapy, we are all in it together. And yes, they will have bad days; so do we. We are all human. It's our responsibility to be there for them through it all.

Aside from our skill, what we do behind the chair is like a calling. And when I find myself overwhelmed with running this business, and I'm losing sight of my mission, I remember what we mean to our people, and it all makes sense. I realize there's a lot more good than bad.

If This Chair Could Talk

The art of hairdressing goes far beyond our skill to create. We are relied upon as a therapist, a social director, and even a fortune teller. It is our job to navigate their moods and turn their day in a positive direction.

Every person who sits in our chair has a story. Some are quite basic, but most are pretty complex. Like a therapist, we are usually privy to their deep dark secrets. It's our responsibility to keep it in the chair and take it to the grave. We know where all of the bodies are buried and all the dirt on the people in their lives. The salon chair is sacred. What is said in the chair stays in the chair. It's our responsibility to not divulge any gossip and ruin their trust. But if it's information that would protect a client from feeling upset in our salon if the topic was brought up, then by all means, we conference in all employees to know what not to say or do.

I made the mistake of upsetting a client very early on in my career. I was just starting out as a shampoo girl, and a client of the salon told us at her last visit that she was finally pregnant after years of trying. She came in two months later, and I felt confident as part of the inner circle, so as I was shampooing her hair, I casually asked her when the baby was due. All of a sudden, she began to cry and was bawling so bad, I had to stop the water to help her up. Little did I know, she had recently suffered a miscarriage, and no one at the salon filled me in on that. Had they told me her heartbreaking secret, I would have known to not say anything about it, but now it was too late.

That day, I learned that although a client's secret should be kept quiet, it is best to update anyone who is present of any client's situation. She's getting a divorce? Talk about a TV show. They lost their job? Discuss the weather. Talk about nail polish color, a recipe—anything to deter from their sad reality that they are coming to us to escape. I learned the hard way when I upset that poor lady, not knowing about her miscarriage. I might know that my client is pregnant, but until they are pushing that baby into my salon in a stroller, I do not ask a peep.

We become contentious bargaining chips in divorces. Who gets custody of the hairdresser when the marriage breaks up. It is a very difficult road to navigate making sure that each party is not present when the other one is in, getting their hair done. Same goes for broken friendships or bad blood between clients. We know it all, and we say nothing. We have to stealthily organize the schedule to avoid traffic jams. Nothing worse than two PTA moms who debate at the school board meetings be present in each other's happy place by getting serviced at the same time. The salon is supposed to be a place to get away from your stress, so it's our responsibility to see to it that there are no obstacles or enemies in their way.

Hairstyling 101

If you are going to create a new style on a client, nine times out of ten, they are not going to be able to recreate it at home. We whip it up and make it look so easy, but when the client is home in their own bathroom with their own tools, they experience frustration as they try to do something new. They have amnesia as to our directions about brush placement or properly sectioning of their hair to execute this new change in style. They'll apply mousse on their dry hair or spray hair spray on their wet hair even when we told them the opposite.

In their defense, they are styling it backward in the mirror, a trait that we have perfected over the years of working in front of one. But to your client, it's all just backward. Any hairdresser would agree if you saw your client outside of the salon in the real world after just giving them a new style, they are probably styling it like their old style, simply because of habit and frustration. It makes you wish you were like Jennifer Lopez in *The Wedding Planner* with a blow-dryer, brush, and some hair spray strapped to your leg so you can grab your client, throw them in a public bathroom, and fix it so your reputation stays intact.

It is said that you need to do something a hundred times for it to become a habit. It is our job to take the time to educate our clients on the new techniques and ways to create their style, so they are 100 percent happy with the finished result and become confident in their own skills. Taking the time to teach them how to style will allow us to maintain them as clients for the long haul. I take my hair down and physically demonstrate on my own head how to get those bangs to stay smooth or how to achieve height on the top of the crown. The client needs to see the placement of our hands, the direction of the blow-dryer, or how we hold the brush to get a true understanding of how to reenact this on their own head.

Our job goes beyond what we can do with scissors. We need to teach a how-to for each client so they can go home and execute the style on their own. I could give you a great haircut, but if you cannot duplicate the style at home, it's a terrible cut. And it's a terrible representation of my hairdresser commitment to a client if I leave them out in the dark.

There are reasons why certain products work for certain parts of any given style. You must use heat protectant if you will be using a blow-dryer or any heat tool. You need mousse or a volumizing root lifter to achieve any form of height in the crown area; otherwise, your hair will fall flat. In order for your hair to lie smooth and straight, you will have to use antifrizz oil, heat-activated straightening product or serum while styling. Your style might require dry shampoo or a texturizing paste in order to give your hair a piecy, lived-in finish. And because I am a girl from the '80s, I believe a little hair spray is necessary to seal the deal.

If your clients walk out without purchasing product from you, especially if they received a new cut or a new color, you clearly did not do your job properly. We are like doctors giving a prescription to our patients. Our tutorial does not stop at skill and technique. Our tutorial must include info about the proper home care so their color doesn't fade, their style stays on point, and they are not buying products that they *think* are good for them from that dangerous aisle in Target. We are their hair gurus, and we will always have the best interest of their hair at heart. Trusting us should be our number 1 goal, and if we can achieve that, the rest is history.

Most clients think they know what they want for a style but truly are indecisive and are just craving something different, not necessarily wanting change, just going through something impactful in their lives that makes them think changing something with their hair will fix the problem. Getting a divorce? Go blonde. Just had a baby? Cut it shorter. Miserable at your job? Get extensions. Money problems? Cut some bangs. These are the signs, and a good hairdresser should know when to pull rank and get to the root of the problem (no pun intended). It is our job to sense the hormonal, emotional, situational requests and really see if they want that change or just a fix to make something better.

That's when I use my Spidey-sense and gauge where this change might be coming from. A client inquires about a random new look. I act slightly indifferent at their idea of change and see if they display any hesitation. If it's a true change that they are craving, they will whip out a Pinterest portfolio of pictures they have researched for this new look and talk me back into it, and I will be happy to oblige. But if they don't, and my instincts were correct, they will back down and confess their woes. Works every time.

A good hairdresser knows their clients and wouldn't just hastily agree to something out of the ordinary or do something they know the client might regret. If you truly have connected with them, they will trust you and let you guide them properly. You two will work together to give them something new and exciting yet appropriate for their needs. It's all about the relationship you build with each individual client, knowing their abilities, lifestyle, financial responsibilities, and emotional state. It doesn't do anybody good to go all in, *Thelma & Louise* style, jumping into a look they will potentially hate just because it's what they asked for.

Many times I've done work that I am not really happy about, but if the client asks for it, really wants it, and is genuinely happy with it, who am I to say it's bad.? But most come to us based on trust, and we need to take that seriously. Because nothing stings more than having to redo that clients hot mess for free, especially when you *knew* it was a bad idea from the start.

Drunk Clients

I'll put this in terms that some of you might understand. Clients are like different types of drunks. There are many ways to classify a drunk, all different types of personalities, and you never really know what type you are dealing with until it's in the moment. You've got blackout drunks, your fun drunk, your emotional drunk, your irresponsible drunk, your passed-out drunk, your hostile drunk, your quiet drunk, your daredevil drunk, your easy-breezy drunk, your indecisive drunk, etc. Minus the alcohol, clients are very much the same.

Sudden amnesia

That home hair color commercial makes it look so easy; how hard can it be? Or why call up the salon and ask to have to have my bangs trimmed, I've had it done so many times I'm sure I can do it. Especially after a glass or two of wine. In that moment of desperation, it always seems like a good idea, until it isn't. The truth is, the way we operate and are able to hold a conversation as we work makes it look so easy that you are convinced it can't be that difficult. It's like watching the Cooking Channel and trying to recreate the moves of the chef as they chop, sauté, and flambé, only to learn how difficult it really is when you chop off half your finger or accidentally burn off your eyebrows while cooking!

Blackout clients only think in the moment and rely on the hope that their faithful hairstylist will overlook their blunder, or rectify the mishap and make everything better. They usually do not confess to any hair crime at first because they conveniently banished the event from their memory yet have a fluttering remembrance of that ill-fated self-bang trim only while we stand in front of them combing this wacky mess in confusion. "Oh, I think I *might've* trimmed my bangs a bit," they say. Even though they swear at first that they did not use a box dye to color their roots, they come clean only because the evidence is clear that they did, as we stand over their foils in a stupor wondering why the color won't lift properly.

As a professional, we are trained to ask a series of questions to be sure that we are on the same page so once the work begins, we do not hit any potholes in the road. But in these cases, a state of amnesia seems to occur and an apparent visit from the hair fairy must've happened while they were sleeping because this type of client cannot seem to recall any incident where they were responsible for this mess.

Fun Betty

Your fun client is always open for something different at each appointment. They are open to new looks and different color ideas and hardly ever get the same thing the next time they see you. They are inspired by your ideas and rely on you to create.

It's fun to have these creative clients because they always put us to the task and keep us on our toes. They will immediately post their new look on social media, probably already taking salon selfies and documenting their visit on Snapchat sitting in your chair. They are trendsetters and self-proclaimed influencers, and they have herds of people who anticipate their changes, who are willing to follow right into your chair, which is a great way to build and increase your clientele.

But it can also be anxiety inducing, hoping this isn't the time you fail them…because all their followers will know.

Evel Knievel

Some fun clients can sometimes be daredevil clients. Daredevils are always fun, but we know every time they are in our schedule, they are definitely going to put our skills to the test. Don't get me wrong.

We love a challenge, but it's hard to determine what creative concoction they've thought up, knowing this will be an intense appointment. You usually see their name in your schedule and have a mini panic attack, hoping that you have the appropriate amount of time put aside and pray you weren't drinking the night before so you will have 100 percent of your strength to strategize their new look.

Most daredevil clients love anything edgy, requesting wildly eccentric hair color or huge amounts of hair to be cut on a whim. They will decide that morning to have long Rapunzel-like hair, investing in thousands of dollars in hair extensions just to take them out by the next appointment to have a radically different short style—anything for shock and awe. Their visits usually are lengthy and almost always requires a nap and a cocktail once completed, mostly for the stylist.

Kitchen beauticians

There is a frustrated hairdresser in everyone. Nothing feels more powerful than standing over someone with sharp implements in your hand, ready to create a masterpiece or, in most cases, a mishap. Kitchen beauticians are like drunks with beer muscles. They feel that since they've seen it done before, by proxy, they surely have the skills to do it to themselves at home. They get caught up in the power and instantly become a balayage expert or haircutting genius. Most of their family members have been the victims of their attempts and hide whenever their mom wants to play beauty parlor in the kitchen.

And as we assess their mess at their next appointment, they stand firm and argue that their work was much better this time.

Yeah, mon

As an easy-breezy drunk might be, we have many clients who allow us free rein to do whatever we see fit. Anything goes because they trust us. We are always their designated driver because we have the license to prove it. We rattle off a few ideas, and they stare blankly in our face, declaring that they don't care. They choose to come to us because we know best.

Blind faith in our skills is the Girl Scout badge of earning their respect. We've always made them happy, they have faith that we know what they need or want, and they rejoice in the fact that they can enjoy a mindless experience because our track record has been good. They trust our recommendations on products to use at home, pay what we charge because they respect our business, and reschedule like champs, knowing the only way to maintain their look is to follow the rules and return. God, if only all of our clients would be so trusting.

The worrier

Your emotional clients will spill out their life story to you, same as they would to a bartender. You know all the names of their family members and their background even if you haven't met them at all. They are known to suffer from buyer's remorse very easily, not always sure if they are happy with their choice. An emotional client might crave a new style, even bring you inspo pictures to communicate, but once it's done, they aren't sure if they like it.

One thing I've learned, people fall in love with the idea of the style they want, but once they see it on themselves, they become unsure. They expect to look exactly like the model, and now it's their own face with the hair in the mirror. It's hard for most people to look beyond that, and now here they are with the exact replica you were able to create to mimic the picture, yet their face hasn't changed, so there is doubt. I tell my clients, "I'm a beautician, not a magician. These are scissors, not a magic wand." I'm sure a great plastic surgeon can make your face similar to the model, but I only do the hair. Once they sober up or get used to the style, they are always okay with it.

Some clients come in so sure of themselves, for instance boldly stating they want four inches cut off the length. After a complete consultation showing exactly where the length will lie, we proceed and then begin to see a change of demeanor. They see this shorter new do, hitting exactly where we told them it would be, and they become silent. The silence is so deafening; it translates to doubt. We know we've explained and visually demonstrated what the end result will be, but seeing it in reality is emotional and shocking for many, so

it takes some time to get used to. A little Xanax doesn't hurt either…
for both of us.

If you sense they are not just emotional, that they are truly
unhappy, don't ever let them leave. Once they pass the threshold of
your door unsatisfied, that's the last you'll ever see if them. But that's
not the last you'll ever hear of them because they will tell everybody
how unhappy they were in their experience and their finished result
from your salon. Pay close attention to their body language, and if
they truly aren't happy, sit them back down and do what you have
to, to rectify. If it looks too light sitting in your chair in the salon, it's
going to look twice as light in their own bathroom mirror. It's worth
running behind in your schedule to accommodate them because they
will always remember that you cared enough to take the time.

"Karen"

Not often, but these emotional clients sometimes turn into
emotionally hostile clients. They ain't happy. A little freaked out, suffering from buyer's remorse. Too light, a bit too short, too flat, too
much money, took too long to do—whatever it is, they claim that's
not what they expected. This is why I encourage clients to bring pictures. It's a mirror to the inside of their head, showing me a definite
image of what they would like me to achieve.

A consultation is necessary with every client, and it reassures
both parties that we are starting off on the same page. It is important
to explain each detail and necessary step to get to this desired style
and give them an idea of how their hair will look or react. I assess
their hair and facial structure carefully to see if the style will be possible with their current hair situation, pointing out any differences
their natural hair might be with the hair of the photo. We talk an
estimate of price and what type of commitment will be needed by
them to incur this new look, inquiring what their skills are and what
kind of effort they are willing to put into their new look. I finish up
the consultation by explaining all the types of styling products and
methods that will be required to execute this style properly. I follow

this script all to avoid disillusion and to cover my ass, so once we begin the service, our seat belts are on, and we are both ready.

I can usually sense who might wind up being hostile or upset. I feel the pushback from my questions, their inability to listen to my educated opinion, or I sense their fear that they might not like it once they see it on themselves. So I refrain from cutting it as short as the picture or won't dye it as dark as the color they choose. I pull back on how chunky or bright those highlights are, and this tactic generally works like a charm.

Looking at something in a picture and seeing it on yourself can be a completely different ball game, and I know from experience that my conservativeness is usually highly appreciated. I can always go back and cut it shorter or add another foil or two if needed. Can't put it back on once it's on the floor being swept away.

Now, some clients are just naturally hostile. I can sense it like a bloodhound. They walk in for the first time, telling you in the first five minutes at least six reasons why they left their last salon. Showing me inspo pictures that are clearly not possible, two of the first questions they ask are the following:

1. How much will this cost?
2. How long will this take?

And immediately, the hairs on my neck stand up. Red flag— this is not going to end well. I do my best to communicate how I can possibly get from point A to point B for this client, and many times, it's a pretty simple plan. Many times, it requires time, and the client might need to spend hours in the chair that day, or it may require a few visits to finally achieve. And unfortunately it will cost a certain amount of money each time.

One of the issues we face today is that social media has made achieving your hair goals seem like a magic trick. Walk in with broken straw-like black-box-color hair, and in two hours' time, you strut out of the salon a beautiful, unbrassy blonde bombshell. It seems so simple, so it must not be too expensive because that Instagram story showed it took no time at all!

Disillusioned they are, what they neglect to realize is that it can take months to achieve the final goal, and yes, it costs a lot to get there in time and money. The post they showed us from Instagram doesn't explain that it took several visits to achieve that before-and-after result. And quite possibly, it's filtered and photoshopped to appear perfect.

But explain that to a potentially hostile client. Nonsense, they say! How long will that take? You must be new at this if you say it will take that long to do. You can't fit me in this Saturday for a five-hour color corrective, balayage, haircut, conditioning treatment, or blowout? I'll just go somewhere else, they say. Bye, I say. Give them Uber fare and walk them to the door.

Digging yourself deeper with someone who's so difficult before your hands even touched them? Recipe for disaster. If they can't understand the process and put their trust in your work, it will never work. Cut your losses and do not commit to them. Being a good hairdresser is having a good shit detector, a sense to sniff out the problem before you even touch their hair. Because trust me, it's never worth it.

Tardy to the party

And we all have them. late for their appointment, with a fresh Starbucks in their hand-Irresponsible Clients. Always with a perfectly well thought out excuse as to why they are late. Of course it's well thought out, it was perfectly concocted while on line at the exact time of their appointment, waiting for their nonfat vanilla latte! They usually refuse to prebook and wind up calling last minute begging for the soonest opening. Like you didn't know those roots were going to be grown in four weeks later…PREBOOK like everyone else!

Most irresponsible clients will think nothing of canceling at the last minute, with a fascinating tale of what occurred to derail their appointment. We have a policy that at five minutes late beyond your appointment time, we call to see if you are en route. There are many occasions that the client clearly forgot, or got caught up and is apologetic, feeling terrible for their mix up. But an Irresponsible Client will answer that call like nothing in the world is wrong. "I'm on my way" they declare, even though it's already eight minutes into their thirty minute appointment. Sometimes they are so irresponsible, they will insist that the appointment is incorrect, it's at a different time/day. Even if they already confirmed via text from the day before! We can't run a successful business and resort to giving each client a one hour-before reminder calls to get in the car and start heading to the salon, although many would like us to do so…What most irresponsible clients don't understand is that due to their absence, we isolated an appointment time for them and turned away other willing clients to commit to their given time. And when they cancel last minute or don't show up there is no way to fill that slot, essentially leaving us with wasted space and a loss of money. Some of the most chronic of cases, we've had to part ways with certain clients because although we love them as people, we know it's a sure sign of disrespect to our profession.

Silence Is golden

Some clients are like quiet, zoned out drunks…Quiet clients are usually our favorite because, duh… But seriously, they are just choosing to unplug and enjoy their experience and revel in the buzz. It might be boring for someone like me, someone in constant conversation all throughout the day. But it allows me the time to regroup myself, focus on the task and just work. But it is imperative that I execute the consultation because they will tune out and I need to be certain I know exactly what they want, so those quiet clients don't find their inner Karen and turn into a hostile client. You know what they say, silent but deadly! Wake up from their slumber and not be happy with the end result, hence migrating into a hostile client. And there's nothing worse than a hostile drunk waking up from a slumber…

Speaking of slumber, we have clients that literally nod off and fall asleep in our chair. Sometimes while we are still working on them! I'm standing behind them, a half hour deep into a foil highlight and boom. their head drops forward and we hear a gentle snore…

Passed out like they had one too many glasses of Pinot Noir. I do agree, nothing feels more relaxing than someone playing with your hair. And most clients come after work, or after running a bunch of errands, so this might be the first time all day they could sit and relax.

We do a nap countdown for one of our clients. She runs a day-care facility and comes in for her color appointment when she's done with work for the day. Without fail, she sleeps throughout her entire color service. Three, two, one…she's out. Head tilted, chin in chest, complete comatose state. Thirty minutes later the timer rings, her eyes open and she says, "I'm done already?"

I love that clients feel so comfortable in our setting that they can actually chill out and rest. I could care less if they take that time to nap, as long as they keep their head still…and keep their snoring to a minimum.

Negative Nelly

We all have that client who is never happy with anything. Out to dinner in a great restaurant, and she hates the food. Go see a new movie, and she hates the actor. Now add in a few drinks, and she's a naggy drunk. No filter, holds back nothing, feels the need to express full brutal honesty.

Try servicing these kinds in your chair. They are never satisfied. You can go out of your way to dazzle these people, but it's never enough. I execute the exact color from the inspo picture that they showed me, and it's too light. I duplicate that supermodel's hairstyle, and it's too poufy. They ask for something different and amazing, and I use up all of my creative juices to do so, and all they can muster as a reaction is "meh". They think nothing of calling me to repair a problem, which always sounds catastrophic. But once I see them in person, you can't quite understand or see what the problem is. The truth is some people, whether sober or drunk, just are not capable of being satisfied. They will always find fault and nitpick on the most minute details. And to a hairdresser who is going above and beyond to make them happy, it's very discouraging. And most times, they do not mean it or realize how negative they actually are. It's a natural way of life for them.

I had a client that regardless of the task, I pulled it off, and she still found fault. Any product recommendation I made, she hated. She wanted me to cut bangs, then she hated them. I gave her advice on how to properly style her hair, and she said it didn't help.

Well, she came in one day when I must've had no patience for it, and the negativity started as soon as she walked in the door. Bitch, moan, hiss—I just wasn't in the mood for it today, so I sat her down. I politely told her that I would have no problem if she decided to go elsewhere for her hair from now on, that I tried endlessly to please her, but her response was always negative. I want her to be happy, but I've exhausted everything I had to try to please her, and she deserves to find someone to help her better than me.

She stared at me shocked and sadly said, "But I love how you do my hair."

I answered, "You love how I make you hate it?"

I think I put her in check, and she immediately apologized and asked to please stay on as a client. I agreed but took the opportunity to express to her all about my exhausted efforts to unsuccessfully make her happy. She listened and was pleasant throughout her service.

When I saw her a few weeks later, she told me that she told her husband what I had said. He was impressed and elated that I discussed my feelings to her because his biggest gripe was her blatant negativity toward everything. And when I asked how her hair was, she proudly answered, "The last cut was amazing!"

See, sometimes a naggy client just needs a little brutal honesty right back at them to make them understand what it's like to receive, and hopefully, they pay attention to how they respond, which makes everything better.

A close call

Like the old saying goes, "You can't make everybody happy." We know that is an impossible task. And some people love to complain;

it's like a sport for some. But if they are truly not satisfied, we need to take that seriously. Just because a client might be complaining doesn't make them a pain in the ass. They are paying a lot of money and choosing you, so it's your duty to rectify any problems to make it right.

A situation occurred with a client whose roots didn't seem to cover very well at that visit. It was the last appointment of the day, and the stylist was rushing to finish and get home. I noticed from working two chairs away that the client was visibly not satisfied at the color job she received. She kept leaning toward the mirror, getting a closer look at the glowing spot. I overheard the client ask the stylist if the roots looked too light, and she replied no and blamed the brightness on the overhead lighting. She then followed it up by telling the client to go home, and if it still felt too light, she could come back that weekend, and she would fix it.

The stylist finished blowing the client's hair and walked away to gather her things to go home for the night. I followed her into the back room and expressed my concern that if she did not stay and fix those roots, that client would never come back. She didn't want to recognize at first that the client was not happy, but at the risk of losing a client, she knew she had to do the right thing and offered to stay and fix it. She quickly went up to the desk and had her client sit back down, and she reapplied a little more color to fix it.

When it was done and corrected, the client was so happy and so grateful that the stylist took the extra time to make it perfect. Even till this day, when I see that client in our salon, she always takes me aside and whispers to me how appreciative she was in regard to how I run my business. She admits if she'd left our salon that evening being as unhappy as she was, that definitely would've been the last time we would've seen her. But we cared enough to stay late and take the time to rectify a problem.

That type of reputation goes for miles because that happy client will tell everyone how we went above and beyond to make sure she left happy. Our name and reputation are on every head we touch, so if it means you have to pull a last-minute redo, then you do it. Yes, it's annoying to have to stay late when you might have plans or be tired from a long day, but it's more annoying to lose clients because you didn't do the right thing.

A happy client is the best advertisement a stylist can get. Each client has at least five people in their lives whom they will either brag or bash your work to. No one can afford to lose a client, especially over something so simple to fix. We should all strive for them to brag.

Prima donna

I had an assistant who previously worked in beauty parlors as an assistant for years. She rushed through her shampoos, wasn't cautious about getting water in clients' ears, and made little attempt to properly remove all color stains from their hairline and faces. I'd conference her from time to time if a client complained, as any good boss would have to do, telling her to try to pay closer attention to providing the clients with a nice experience.

In return, she told me that all of my clients were a bunch of spoiled prima donnas, and I agreed. I told her exactly how I expect all of my customers to be treated. Give them the best service you can and make sure everyone leaves happy. I don't expect my assistants to just wash hair. I expect them to give my clients a true relaxing experience. We value their loyalty and continued patronage and provide them with the utmost care while in our salon at all levels possible. So if they like ten extra seconds of a head massage while getting shampooed, so be it. If they like having coffee served to them while they are sitting, getting a color process, why would I say no? Clients appreciate when the assistant removes all residue of color from their faces after completing their wash at the sink. I don't think that makes them difficult. Our clients pay our bills and keep the lights on in our salon. If it wasn't for those prima-donna clients, we would have no business to run. I have never viewed our clients as spoiled. I just know how I would like to be treated and treat them accordingly. A client makes a conscious decision to choose us for their beauty needs. They can go anywhere they want, so we want to show them our thanks in any way possible, and anyone who can't understand how to follow those simple rules can't work for this bossy prima donna!

Some of the people who sit in my chair consider our staff as family or as a big part of their inside circle. They confide in us things they might not have told their own family. It's our job to be compassionate but still professional. As a silent hairdresser oath, what is said in the chair stays in the chair. They might feel comfortable telling me their deep, dirty secrets, but once they leave, it stays in the vault.

It's amazing to see the relationships that build between our clients. They find themselves on the same schedule and rotation in the salon, receiving services every few weeks, quickly becoming old-school beauty-parlor friends! It's wonderful to see the connections our clients/family make simply just existing in our little cocoon. Recipes and restaurant recommendations are shared, Netflix series discussed, child rearing advice given. It's a cool thing to have this coffee-klatch feel, everyone joining in to be one big happy family, similar to the hair version of the show *Cheers*. And yes, true to form, we hairstylists are the bartenders.

But there are moments when it is not always such a joyous event. I glance ahead to our schedule and see that Mrs. Jones's *ex*-daughter-in-law is due in at the same time as her estranged mother-in-law, which means we have to swiftly act to rearrange appointments so a massive traffic jam does not occur.

As for the bartender aspect of our role, we know most of the dirty secrets among our clients. The broken friendships, failed marriages, which PTA moms cannot play nice in the sandbox—you name it, we know it. It's imperative to reach out to someone in that situation and alert them that they might be at the salon with their former BFF or estranged sister-in-law. We allow them the courtesy to rearrange their appointment to avoid this situation.

Under no circumstance will I ever allow a client to feel uncomfortable in our salon, and if I have quick intel that there might be a collision in the making, I feel it's my duty to make accommodations. Anyone who chooses my salon deserves to have a pleasant, happy experience. It's not their fault that this happens, but I feel it is my duty to make sure it doesn't. No one should endure their services with a knot in their stomach. We are all human, and we are not going to get along with everyone. But the last thing I want is both Mrs.

Jones and the former Mrs. Jones Jr. to feel uneasy in our environment because although they were once family, this situation could be awkward.

Sometimes two clients are gabbing away, name-dropping, and unleashing some juicy gossip, unaware that the other client sitting a few feet from them knows exactly who they are talking about. It is easy to get caught up in the conversation and forget your surroundings, but remember, we are all six degrees of separation from each other. You might not know them, but for instance, your sister-in-law might be their neighbor.

We had a situation occur years ago during a busy Saturday morning. We were accommodating one of our clients on her wedding day. Her entire bridal party and future in-laws were there to be serviced that day, getting ready for the big wedding. The groom's two sisters were present and were purposely conversing in Greek so neither the bride nor her friends would understand the rude conversation they were engaging in, mostly about their dislike for their brother's future bride.

Well, wouldn't you know it, a client in the salon, who was not part of this group, was quietly waiting for her color to process and happens to be native *Greek!* She understood every vile word they were saying and was disgusted at their rude behavior. She took pity on the bride, knowing the snarky things these evil stepsisters were saying. As she was leaving, she walked over to the bride, congratulated her on her big day, then quietly explained her intel. The bride was embarrassed yet not shocked, explaining that these sisters had been so difficult from the start. As the client was leaving, she walked past the two evil sisters-in-law and told them in Greek that they should be more respectful to the bride on their brother's wedding day. *Busted!*

So moral of the story: it doesn't matter what language you speak. Do not talk mean about anyone. That's bad Karma. *Someone* will always hear it.

Dinosaurs Versus Avatars

When I started in this industry thirty-five years ago, it was the bridge of time between a beauty parlor turning into a beauty salon. The smell of lacquer and perms permeated through the air, big hard-cover-style books sitting on a coffee table right next to the cigarette ashtray to help inspire clients looking for a new style.

Highlights were known as frostings, a rubber cap placed on a person's head with a small crochet needle used to pluck the hair through a small hole. As painful as you could imagine, yet all the rage back then in a beauty parlor setting. Everyone paid in cash because the credit card machine was a carbon-copy contraption and hardly ever used. Most everyone was a regular, most from the neighborhood coming in for their weekly appointments, like they were walking into the bar on *Cheers*. Inspiration pics were torn-out pages from a magazine, and no service was complete without a dust cloud of hair spray sealing in your do. Hair products were bought from your local salon, not online because that didn't exist yet. There was no such thing as social media—no Instagram or Pinterest to inspire your looks, no TikTok or YouTube to try to figure out how to do it yourself.

I was what is referred to as a homegrown stylist. I was in ninth grade when I began working in a salon, so I started out as a shampoo girl without any skill or formal training. I actually lied in my interview that I was currently enrolled in the cosmetology program in my high school just because I wanted the job, even though I wouldn't start the program until my junior year two years from then. I was mentored and trained as I went, I learned by watching and assisting the stylists. I still believe this was the best education a newcomer can get.

These days, stylists get a license after finishing cosmetology school and learn a lot of their skills virtually from what they watch on social media. They choose not to start out their careers working as an assistant in a salon, where they would have started out from the bottom, missing out on all of that hands-on wisdom doing an apprenticeship. Instead, they rent salon suites, essentially working alone all day, hindering their ability to learn from others. More importantly, they miss out on mastering the art of socialization by not working alongside other people.

Not that I have anything against salon suites, but for a beginner in this industry, that is not a way to grow and gather a clientele. Starting as a homegrown in my very first salon job, I was able to prove to all of the salon clients that I had a good work ethic, showcasing my skills and already making connections with them by simply washing their hair. When the stylists would go on vacation or were out on maternity break, the clients gladly came to me, knowing by their observation of me that I was qualified and able to accommodate them.

Building a clientele was an easy task in that forum. I didn't have to seek it out because it was right there. Even though I might not have been as qualified being a new hairdresser, the relationship I built at the sink made them comfortable enough to trust me. Those who do not have the luxury of starting from the bottom like I did do not grow as quickly. They have to seek out clients, relying on social media to do the work for them. And without any human connections, it becomes an impossible mission. You can't sit around all day assuming clients will find you as you hang alone in your suite. Being in a salon setting with an audience of clients to perform for its a recipe for growth and success, a platform to show off your talented work. Dressing the part, looking and acting professional, gave clients the confidence to trust me.

Being by yourself, working alone in a salon suite kind of feels sad to me. There's no workplace camaraderie to build, friendships to begin with coworkers, and in those moments of despair, there is nobody there to help "think tank" your strategy when having a client dilemma. In a salon, we all work off of each other and have the luxury to go into the back room and be able to ask your peers how to figure out a hair problem. I worry what stylists who work alone in a salon suite do when they have nobody but themselves to figure it out. No one to casually walk past the head in question to sneak a glance and assess the quandary to help out their team member. I love having a team around me. We work better because we work together, and it all adds to the feeling of success.

I know that any new stylist of today is fueled by what they are learning on social media, which, to even a dinosaur like me, I will agree has inspired me and has put a little more drive into my tired old hands. Balayage techniques, customized color, new products, all different phases of hair extensions, fancy formal styling—there's an educational reel of just about anything to learn from. But don't forget, they all have photoshopped filters and time-lapse options to make it all appear to be easy.

Ask these newcomer stylists how to properly wrap a perm rod—impossible! Like the old state board exam where old-school finger waves and pin curl sets are still included, these are techniques that you need to learn early on to help groom your skills for later. The skill of finger dexterity to properly roll the hair around the perm rod, the tension you need to wrap that rod so it will allow the hair to chemically expand during processing. How to work quickly to keep your timing right. To make each perm rod line up perfectly in a row to achieve a uniformed wave. It might seem prehistoric to some, but all of that old-school training from back then has helped me behind the chair till this very day.

As antiquated as teaching a perm technique might seem these days, it's the lesson of consistency, technique, and coordination that these basic old skills teach for further development. And wouldn't you know it? Old things do come back around. Just recently, young high-school-age boys are actually requesting to have perms for their mop-top styles! Imagine a new stylist getting a request to do a perm. They'll freeze like a deer in the headlights! Good thing this old dinosaur has the ability to do it, so these new stylists can go breathe into a paper bag as I complete the process. Modern medicine might teach a new doctor how to robotically fix an organ, but basic skill can teach him to cut through the skin to get to it first. It is always a good foundation to start from the beginning, doing actual hands-on work, figuring out how to get from point A to point B.

There is all this talk about AI and how it's a revolutionary new approach in an attempt to change the hairdressing field as we know it. That might be true because like everything else in this life, you have to roll with the new times and adapt to the technology in order to strive. But AI, which stands for artificial intelligence, is just that—artificial. No amount of AI could replace the hands of a human physically creating a style on a client's head. Yes, it's a unique approach to business development, but it all seems inauthentic, generating a look that was put together by a bot, not a stylist, which is inevitably setting us up for disappointment because like everything else of today, it's feeding into all of the instant gratification that technology makes us believe. To expect that exact result because that's what the picture shows. Taking the easy way out and letting a computer generate our social media postings without our own creative spark behind it. It's just one more way to stifle our imagination by letting a computer do the work.

What we are lacking today is the personalization of one-on-one human contact. Our lives are so dialed in these days, with everything done by our devices, that it seems so disconnected from reality. Just google it and let your device find it for you. Advertising was so organic without all of this technology. It was mostly word of mouth, a genuine recommendation from a happy client. I still have those old-school values, and as much as I know I will get in line and adapt to the new technology to some degree, we are still a people business. I stand firm on hairstyling to be one of the last occupations that requires the hard work and skill of an actual human being. This is not the futuristic world of Judy Jetson, pressing a button and a device instantly styles your hair. Now if AI can supply me with Rosey the Robot to instantly clean my salon all day long, then sign me up!

Watching hairstyling, color, balayage, or highlight tutorials on Instagram has been a great tool for me to reinvent my techniques and work off of the basic methods that I learned years ago. Since COVID-19 occurred, there have not been as many hands on hair workshops to attend as there were in the past, so all of these social media options are a godsend for a willing stylist. I can watch a five-minute reel and instantly learn something new. I'll observe new products to use, foil placements to try, and application techniques I never thought of. Had this been available earlier in my career, I would've been up every night till 3:00 a.m., falling down the hair-tutorial rabbit hole, learning anything and everything I could. I see how inspired I am now, how psyched I get to do that new technique I learned on TikTok on my next client.

But as informative as these videos try to be, many are altered to jump to the end result without really showing the journey. The faces are filtered to look like perfect avatars, a lot of the physical work is cropped out, and some of the finished product is filtered. It is hard to tell what is raw or enhanced. Miraculously, no one has acne or cellulite, and their waists are perfectly cinched. Their lips and lashes are on point, and the hair is always perfect, sometimes with a halo of flowers floating above their heads. It is very misleading to some who see these images and think it is easy or that the impossible is possible.

A seasoned stylist can pick up little tips and figure out the rest by already having some knowledge and experience. My fear is that a newcomer, without having much physical experience, will feel blindly confident watching a tutorial but become discouraged when they attempt to perform it and realize it is not as easy to accomplish as it seems. We were all inexperienced beginners at one time. I became great at what I do because unfortunately, I did some crappy work in the beginning of my career, and I learned from those experiences. I gained confidence to learn from my mistakes and excel.

But unfortunately I'm not seeing that same level of confidence with this up-and-coming generation. As I converse with my current young assistants, I realize their biggest fear is making a mistake and the client not being satisfied. It is hindering them from trying to grow and giving them the feeling that they will ultimately fail. There is a level of anxiety and a need to be perfect that I'm having a hard time understanding. The thought of rejection or failure is crippling to them, and if they are not 100 percent certain it will be a success, they will quit and not even try to work it out.

There is absolutely no drive from this younger generation of stylists to physically gain clients or promote themselves unless it's fabricated on social media. Hand out a business card and strike up casual conversation to a stranger as you promote your budding hair career? Absolutely not! Just the thought of that will paralyze them with fear. They will lock themselves in the bathroom to find a safe space to calm down from a panic attack for being pushed to succeed.

Social skills are mandatory in our line of work. Unfortunately for them, this craft that we provide *is* face-to-face with actual people. You can't dial it in. Your smartphone is not going to perform that balayage for four hours; you are! With a living, breathing client, who might actually want to have a conversation with you during that service. You have to physically touch people's hair and work six inches from their head, so basic social skills need to be applied, and human interaction is necessary. Building a clientele is 50 percent technical skill and 50 percent personality. You can be robotic in your work, but you must be a human while you do it.

And yes, it will not be perfect the first time. It never is. But you learn from your mistakes, and you get better with experience. And yes, the client might not be 100 percent happy with the end result. As a stylist, it is very important to build up an emotional callus to protect yourself from unsatisfied customers and strive to fix it and make them happy. Take a deep breath and map it out.

- Step 1, learn what you client wants.
- Step 2, figure out your plan on how you get there.
- Step 3, be patient with yourself; be confident in your work.
- And step 4, if they are not happy, you do everything in your power to fix it.

Remember, fail to plan, plan to fail.

I'm at this thirty-five years, and of course I still make mistakes. I'm human, and I've learned everything I know by doing it wrong at first. I don't call them accidents. I call them discoveries. I discovered that plan was not a good idea and learn never to do it again. Rejection and the feeling of failure are normal when you work in a service business, and it is a humbling lesson to be learned at any age. The difference between an old dinosaur like me and a fine-tuned young avatar of today is that negativity bounces off of me like Teflon, and it makes me work harder to make it better, fueling me for success. This newer generation cannot bear it. They will crumble if they fail and will abandon ship for a new career path to avoid this situation in the future.

I will always treasure my early career experience. Even though I was only the assistant, I was part of the process. Watching someone walk in looking a certain way, observing the ripped-out magazine picture they wanted the stylist to create, and helping along the way as magic was created. It was then that I realized in order to achieve the look, each client has their own individual point A to point B, point A meaning, what does their current hair look like? And point B, how do we get there?

Gray percentage, starting base color, texture, length, thinness or thickness of hair, the client's skill—all of these factors are essential to determine how we can achieve their goal. A lot of times, it is not possible. Clients have a funny habit of choosing a style that their hair cannot achieve. For example, a person with lifeless thin hair asking to have wild curly hair like Debra Messing via *Will & Grace* or someone with wiry coarse hair assuming she can walk out the same day with shiny straight Kim Kardashian hair.

It's not fun breaking the hearts of our trusting clients by telling them that it is not possible, but the worst thing a stylist can do is overpromise, giving unrealistic expectations. The connection you make with your client, the trust they build in your skills, helps ease the heartbreak, and you both work together to achieve something close that their hair will allow.

All of this at the beginning of my career molded me into the type of hairdresser I am today. I firmly believe those earlier years when I assisted and learned on the job were the essential tools I needed to build good communication skills with people in my chair. Sure, you can work really hard on your hairdressing skills and become the best at it, but the art of connecting with people is a far greater skill to achieve. Those earlier years of being the sole assistant for a salon of five hairdressers gave me the ability to absorb every bit of talent from each stylist and connect with each client. That would never have happened if I didn't start from somewhere, and it all came from my start, witnessing the stylists above me do it every day. Whether it was a success or a failure, it was still education. You learn from others' mistakes and always remember it when it's you in the driver's seat. And when you find yourself in a dead end with an unpleasant result, it's the memory of how your superiors handled their trauma, and you navigate accordingly.

I firmly believe I've learned everything I know by screwing it up one time or another. And if it wasn't me screwing it up, I learned from someone else's mistake. It's the art of what *not* to do.

I'm all about the "work smarter, not harder" vibe most have these days. But unless you worked hard enough to build your career up to the level of cruise control, where you can finally take your foot off the gas and work at an easier pace, it's not smart at all. When you achieve the level of success where you are high in demand, allowing you to pick and choose the work that makes you happy, *then* you can proudly say you're in the smart lane. Young aspiring baby stylists can't coast into that lane until they have years of skilled work under their belt to decide who they want to work on or what type of work fulfills them. They have to fail to succeed and earn their stripes to be at that level. Unless they worked through those mistakes and hard times, they haven't earned their seat at the table. They want to start up in this field as a *hair boss*, expecting to cruise before they ascend. I blame this headspace on the everyone who gets a trophy moment, which, in my opinion, was a failed science experiment. Positive reinforcement is always encouraged, but proudly displaying your kid's ninth-place ribbon sets them up for disappointment. Not everyone is given the right to be first place; it's a grueling battle to the top with amazing rewards once earned. Unfortunately, we will all have to agree to disagree about this concept, but I know deep in my heart that my level of success and where I'm at in this industry is so much sweeter because of my hustle. I've reached cruising altitude, and aside from all of the salon ownership responsibilities I have, I earned the ability to work smarter and filter out the headaches to make my life easier.

When I think of all of the money I spent on print advertising when I opened my salon eighteen years ago, it makes my head spin. Before the art of social media, how else could you propel your image and get your name out there unless you paid to put ads in local newspapers and participate in neighborhood advertising. I invested in Welcome Wagon programs, mailed out postcard ads, paid tons of money for weekly ads in our popular town paper, even did a short commercial on News 12, and not one person did we gain from any of it.

The one concept I never entertained was advertising via Groupon, which was a discounted prepaid coupon program where you basically give your services away for a dime. Advertising on Groupon was widely considered a funeral for your business, one last desperate attempt before possible closing. If you had to resort to that, you might as well shut your doors. Groupon consumers weren't looking to find a new salon to stay with. They were looking for discounted services until the next Groupon deal came around.

I don't know about you, but I have always wanted to build a clientele that appreciated my work, understood my business practice, and respected that there is a price to our style of professionalism, not a clientele based on wanting a half-price haircut who would leave you when the next deal came around. As the old saying goes, "you get what you pay for." Most businesses are giving you the bottom of the barrel if you paid via Groupon. You're not getting the number 1 operator with that discount. You're getting a haircut from the shampoo assistant! Who gets a Groupon for Botox or for a keratin treatment? You might as well let your eight-year-old kid drive you to that service. It's comparable to that!

We received a lot of positive feedback from our ads but only from existing clients who were excited to see them. Now enter into the social-media world of Facebook, Yelp, Instagram and other outlets. *Boom!* Overnight return and all free advertising. Social media platforms are a tremendous way to showcase your work and gain the support of followers, who tune in just to see what you will post next—all of this exposure right at your fingertips. It's a time-consuming chore because you have to remain current and stay on top of posting, but it can help a business flourish without spending a dime.

Prom Drama

The prom—my least favorite time of the year. There, I said it.

That somewhat magical time at the end of the school year when teenagers get all gussied up to experience what they think will be the best night of their lives. I can't stop laughing at the thought of that because it couldn't be further from the truth. Don't get me wrong; it's a great time and a nice send-off before these kids branch out into college life. But the best night of their life? Talk to them in ten years. I'm sure they would all agree it was not.

Not to sound too cynical, but in my opinion, the prom is highly overrated, very expensive, and pretty stressful with all the effort that goes into that one day. Delusional students dreaming up the ideal scenario where they will have the perfect date and the perfect dress, hair, and makeup as they transform themselves into red-carpet royalty for the night. You create over thirty years of prom hair, and you'd feel the same way that I do.

So much has changed from the early '90s when I had my prom till now. It used to be so carefree, we put together our own look from an inspiration we saw from the prom issue of *Seventeen* magazine, maybe borrowed a dress from an older sister, and enjoyed a night out with friends. But now? It's like getting ready for the Oscars—glam squad, entourage, and all.

Each prom girl is accompanied by their helicoptering prom mom, who most certainly will stand right over our shoulder, observing every single bobby pin that was placed. I'd bump into them as I'd reach for a tool, and they'd be completely oblivious that they were clearly in my dance space. Parents have no idea the force field they have, how the kids feed off of their presence, and how tough it is to have them around in that crucial moment.

Imagine I'm hard at work duplicating the exact picture that my prom girl showed me. She's happy so far with what I'm creating, calm and fully at ease with her choice and trusting my work. Mom walks over, looks at her in my mirror, and all she has to say is, "Is that what you wanted?"

Instant tragedy! The kid gets uptight, yells at the mom to go sit down, but then starts to doubt my work. I'm 90 percent done, and now the kid might want to change it. Impossible! That day can be so stressful for us to complete that I've had my husband take off from his own job on prom day so like a bouncer, he could control the moms from getting in our way and upsetting their kids.

I have always treasured my memories from my proms. As much as I sound negative about them, they were very special times, and I'm glad I experienced them. Back in my day, a guy in your math class passed you a folded-up note, asking you to prom, or maybe he asked you in the hallway on your way to your next class. We went to the prom in a dress that you bought at the local mall, an itchy monstrosity made up of satin and sequins that, for sure, at least four other girls would also be wearing. You did your own hair, scrunched up that frizzy perm, maybe swept back one side with a decorative to comb to match your tacky dress. You wore dyeable satin shoes that were uncomfortable and never quite matched, and you and your date coordinated the colors for his boutonniere and for your wrist corsage. Makeup was done by yourself with all of the finest cosmetics that CVS could supply.

Most proms were held in your high school gym, which you took part in decorating. There was usually a theme to the night, and you and your school friends worked together to adorn the gym like it was a ballroom, carefully hiding any remnant of physical education.

When the night was over, you dropped off your disposable camera at the CVS one-hour photo, waiting anxiously to see the memories you captured from the night before. Of course, to your dismay, majority of those pictures were poorly lit, out of focus, or you accidentally cut people's heads off. Salvaging what you could from those blurry pics, you put them in a small decorative album that you would tote around in your large pocketbook next to your oversized can of Shaper hair spray. You would whip out that album and show everyone that fabulous night to remember.

The proms of today…well, they are a little different. Let's start with the *promposal.* An elaborate plan needs to be in effect to ask your date to the prom. Roses scattered all over her bedroom, spelling out, "Will you go to the prom with me?" in rose petals on her mattress. Or the guy showing up to your after-school job or your lacrosse practice dressed in a tuxedo, with a long-stem rose, asking you to be his date for the prom. Apparently, this grand gesture is necessary to secure a date even if the couple had been dating for a while.

Now, the dress. The dress store Pzaz doesn't exist anymore, thank God, but the girls of today wouldn't dream of going somewhere so simple. Skimpy, revealing bodycon dresses, most of them custom-made for the event, are what is worn. I didn't know what double-sided tape was until I was about thirty, but these young babes learn really early because a lot of that is used to hold their bodies into their dresses. Strappy diamond-crusted Manolo Blahnik heels chosen as their glass slippers, and the outfit is complete. And once they committed to a dress, they take a selfie of themselves and post it on social media so no one in their grade would dare to get the same dress.

Makeup is done professionally, contouring every single detail and airbrushed to perfection. And as for the hair, after months of discussion and two to three trial runs to be sure it's the most absolutely perfect style, they arrive to the salon—entourage in tow, as if it's their wedding day—to get pretty. Parents hire a professional photographer to come to the house for a photo shoot so they can have their own album of perfect photos of their prom queen to post on their Facebook page. And any pictures taken during that night by the prom attendees are cropped, Facetune filtered, and immediately posted on social media in real time.

One would say that prom season is big business for a salon, and I will admit that it is. Hair being done in one chair, makeup being applied in another. Operators running from girl to girl like a red-carpet glam squad. Parents spare no expense when it comes to glam for their kids. They'll pay for just about anything to make them the most beautiful girl of the night.

But it has become more of a dramatic wedding day experience than it needs to be. I have brides who wouldn't dream of doing more than one hair trial! Airbrushed makeup and huge lashes? They have the most perfect youthful skin and naturally long lashes. Why the necessity? Custom-made scantily clad dresses? They won't be able to sit without their private parts coming undone from the double-sided tape! I can tell you from being an experienced heel wearer that *any* high-heeled shoe will hurt their inexperienced feet. They don't need $650 heels that they will most definitely be taking off and putting on sneakers under their dress. And so what if someone else is wearing the same dress? Why the need to expose your look on social media months before. What ever happened to the element of surprise? And who doesn't love a showdown of Bitch Stole My Look? And to change out of that ensemble midway through the night into a completely different outfit the minute the formal prom event is over?

Maybe I'm just getting too old for this. Every year, I see the prom season getting more and more intense, and after it's all said and done, they will enjoy it just as much as I did when it was my prom, just in a less-itchy dress.

All in all, it is a rite of passage that I am humbled to be a part of. I'm in awe of how sophisticated these girls look and so happy to be a part of their special day. It adds to the roster of special memories I share with each of these girls. Some sat in my chair for their first haircuts, and many I eventually took care of for their weddings. It's this cycle of life that I'm most proud of, being present for these moments, being their person to go through all of these occasions with them, hopefully with their mom sitting in the distance on their best behavior.

Strictly Business

We stand behind the chair for one reason and one reason only—to make people happy. It is no easy task, but any good, reputable stylist knows a happy client is the best advertisement. But a plan of structure needs to be put into play to make that happen. As happy an atmosphere that we aim to provide, rules and boundaries need to be set for clients to ensure everyone plays nicely in the salon sandbox and so business can go on as planned.

Prebooking

You want to be certain to get an appointment at the time and day you want? Book ahead. Unless you like to play Russian roulette and take a chance that something that will fit perfectly in your schedule will magically appear. The odds will probably not be in your favor. Just prebook; stop the insanity! You know that within three to four weeks, those pesky roots will appear, and you will need it anyway. Got an invitation to a function? Book ahead and secure your appointment to ensure you look your best in public. These days, so many people are working from home and have gotten thrown off kilter by not seeing others on a regular basis. But don't you have mirrors in your house? I'm sure you will walk past one and realize you are almost overdue.

I tell my clients to book their next appointment, and if something arises, they can always cancel or reschedule. Sometimes it can even work out as a swap. There might be someone who really wanted that specific time and day but had to choose another date by default. The odds are that I can put them in your appointment time and offer you theirs. And then everyone's happy. I cannot give you an appointment out of thin air, but if you already have a spot, it can be a bargaining chip and work to your advantage. Our work schedules usually resemble a game of Tetris. Move her appointment an hour later, shift that one earlier, see if he can move to a different day, etc.—all to make everything fit like a perfect puzzle piece.

Every so often, a client calls in a panic, insisting that they desperately need to get in on a specific date and will actually have the gall to ask if I could move someone to accommodate them instead. Can you believe the nerve? Not even if you were having lunch with Beyoncé would I move an already-scheduled client who understands the rules and values my craft and booked ahead. But, boy, do they try. I try my best to accommodate them as I can, and I usually pull through. Appointments are handled in a first come, first served manner. No one will ever be pushed aside to satisfy someone else's needs.

Our salon is in the same building as a tennis club. One of my clients—whom I love dearly, and I laugh at her humorous shame—always seemed to forget to book ahead. When put on the wait list for whatever date/time she was hoping for, she joked that she was going to wait in the parking lot on that day at the time she wanted and run over anyone she saw walking toward the building without a tennis racket! Clearly, she figured if they were not there to play tennis, they must be coming to get their hair done! She said she would run in and say the person who had an appointment told her they couldn't make it but to take their spot instead! Obviously that never happened, but this funny lady has finally learned to book ahead.

Nonrefundable deposits

In order to run a business efficiently, it is imperative to secure a nonrefundable deposit for lengthy, intricate salon services. It secures the appointment time that is allotted, and once completed, it is used to pay toward the rest of the balance due. If you are really serious about your visit and have no intention on canceling, there should not be an issue. If you happen to cancel within forty-eight hours of the appointment, you will, unfortunately, forfeit your deposit. Time is money in a salon setting, and we commit a lot of that to you. We are holding a large chunk of time aside to properly execute your service, thus refusing many other clients to be service during that time. If you cancel last minute, we are stuck with free time that we cannot fill at the last minute because we turned away many potential clients to commit to your time slot, unfortunately leaving us with no income that day.

I've always considered a requested deposit to hold a large appointment like going through the TSA security checkpoint at the airport. If you have nothing to hide, why would you care about removing your shoes and allowing TSA officers to scan your body? If you have no plans of canceling, why would you mind paying the deposit?

I can spot a chronic canceller a mile away. If they are not willing to accept the terms and refuse to pay a deposit, they are definitely going to consider canceling down the road. If they do not agree to pay a deposit, it shows they do not respect your time or your skill, displaying no regard to your business. You turned away other clients to make them a priority. Sure, things happen at the last minute that might cause you to have to cancel. You wake up not feeling good, you got called into work, there's a family emergency, your car broke down—yada yada. Unfortunately, these things happen, and we can't predict it. But if something arises and it's not a life or death situation, you will think differently about canceling if you have already invested in your appointment.

Many times, when a client has canceled, we have shown mercy and compassion because we are human after all. It must be a valid reason if they had no choice but to cancel, right? Then you find yourself scrolling on social media later that day and see that the canceller was out later that same evening, clinking champagne glasses with friends, or went away for the weekend instead. It's a miracle! Their kids are miraculously feeling better, or their migraine must've gone away because that's the excuse they used that morning when canceling at the last minute.

I've been in this business long enough to know who my chronic cancellers are, and I keep a mental note as to the nature of their reason, knowing that they can't repeat that excuse ever again! How many times can your grandmother die? Car trouble again? Girl, take an Uber. Bottom line, it is an irresponsible business move to *not* protect our valuable time by requiring a deposit for certain services. Our time and commitment to you are serious, and all we expect is for a client to take our time as seriously as we do theirs.

Lateness

For the love of God, please be on time. Even five minutes late will throw our schedule off for the next client.

I'm slightly neurotic about lateness, especially in my salon. In my opinion, on time is five minutes before your scheduled appointment time. Enough time to check in, take off your coat, use the restroom, and be ready for your service. I feel that lateness is a disease. All it takes is a client showing up five minutes late, and it can throw off our schedule for the rest of the day. And honestly, in a forum like ours, it shows blatant disregard for our time and business. Sometimes it's an issue of traffic, and the client calls from the road to let us know that they will be late, which we understand completely. But most of the time, it's a few minutes past the appointment time, and we resort to calling them, only to be told that—surprise, surprise—they are running late. In the world of technology, there is absolutely no reason you couldn't call to let us know. You don't even have to dial. Isn't that what Siri is for?

Some clients are so chronically late, we will rearrange the schedule without their knowledge, knowing damn well they will not be present at their scheduled time, so we shift it later so we don't get backed up. If I had to do that for every client, I would've had to close my doors a long time ago. We schedule your appointments so precisely and allow the appropriate amount of time to properly complete your service to be ready for the next person exactly on time all day long, so when you show up seven minutes late with a fresh Starbucks, on your phone, needing to use the bathroom before we start, you are only going to piss us off, and that is certainly not a very good idea when sharp implements or toxic chemicals are going to be used on your head. The least you could've done was bring us a doughnut.

Now, like any service business, we might be running late for you. One rule I follow in my salon is to give the client a heads-up call to let them know not to rush in the event that we are running behind. This way, you don't have to stress in case you were anxiously trying to get to us on time. Maybe you can run that overdue errand or even stop to get a latte. Either way, it's just common courtesy to let you know. Some services take a bit more time than expected, so it's only fair that we clue you in. I'm like JetBlue. I might start you a few minutes late, but I'll get you done on time! If we expect you to be punctual, you should expect the same from us.

Price increases

No one likes when prices go up. Gas, groceries, airline tickets, college tuition—I think we are all in the same boat when it comes to this. But unfortunately, it's bound to happen. I see prices of supplies increase every time I look at an invoice. Salaries must go up due to cost of living. The monthly rates for phone, insurance, security, and all other business expenses have increased tremendously. And with that, so must our salon prices. We try our best to be as gentle as possible when a price increase needs to happen, but in order to deliver the top-quality work we have always given, something's gotta give.

We do not charge as much as other salons in our area, but I feel we give good value for what we charge. When you are in our salon, you are receiving the best quality care you can get. I spare no expense on the hair-care products we use and the services we offer. Most salons sell high-end products at their retail display yet use generic Queen Helene shampoo at the sink. Not under my roof. We practice what we preach. I've worked in other salons where they buy those cheap gallons and insist we pour that into the high-end bottle and pretend that is what we are using and want us to persuade you to purchase the real thing to take home, which is why I don't. Authenticity is key. Quality is quality.

My hairdressers and I are always learning, trying to find new, creative trends and innovative products to deliver you the best we can. Our free time is spent honing in on our skills, researching new products and techniques, all to keep your hair the best it can be. No one leaves our chair without helpful tips on how to style, without a recommendation of products to maintain the life span of our work at home, or without feeling like they had an amazing, genuine experience. We provide value to our services. Our investment in our craft deserves what we charge, and our clients respect that. Hair is never a cheap commodity, and to keep you looking as good as you do in and out of our salon, there will always be a price for that.

Tipping

A tip is a gratuity for a job well done. A tip should never be expected. You do good work, you get a tip. You go above and beyond and the client sees that, they tip you more. You do a half-assed job, you get them soaked, and they didn't enjoy the experience, you deserve nothing. These are my rules, and no one is to ever leave my salon without feeling satisfied.

A client sat in my chair after getting washed and confided to me that the washing she just had was the worst shampoo experience she ever experienced. The assistant not only got her shirt and her ears wet, the water was too cold, and she was a bit too rough and too busy talking to someone else the entire time, not paying attention to the person whose head was in the sink. I apologized for the subpar experience and instructed the client not to tip her.

Astounded, she claimed she felt terrible to do that, thinking she is supposed to tip the shampoo assistant regardless. I outright refused to let her leave a tip and explained to her that a tip is a gratuity for a job well done, and she did not experience a job well done. I explained that the only way this assistant will understand that she did a sucky job is to feel it in her pocket.

When she left, the assistant came right up to me and whined that my client didn't leave her a tip, and I had to explain to her why. Just because you did the job doesn't mean you get paid for it. All clients are to be taken care of properly, and you do not get rewarded if it wasn't done to satisfaction. She was annoyed, but I think she finally understood because her work started to improve, and she focused more on the person she was working on. And she saw her tips increase, and then everyone was happy.

Client Interpretations

One of the hardest tasks to accomplish is making a client's vision a reality. With their expectations high, I try very hard to decipher their desired look while also realizing that this look might not be the best idea for them for many various reasons.

As a stylist, it is our job to be up-front and honest with clients if their expectations are set too high and explain all of the reasons why this look might not be able to happen. It might be something they need to work toward and achieve after a few visits, but it might also not be realistic or a good choice for them, their budget, or their lifestyle. So here I am, the Grim Reaper, squashing your fantasy with reality…but hopefully with alternative solutions. It's the mark of a good hairdresser, knowing when it's not a good idea for the client. If we venture down that road and it comprises the integrity of their hair, whose fault is that? Or if we know that their hair will not style like the picture they show us, but we do it anyway just to make them happy, who is responsible when they are miserable? The one with the sharp scissors—guilty as charged.

I vowed never to be pushed to do work that makes my stomach hurt. And by that I mean my "stylist alarm" is sounding off, giving me that inner nauseous feeling, telling me this is only going to end badly…for me *and* for the client.

As already discussed, it is sometimes hard to execute a certain look from the filtered and photoshopped pictures clients show us. They are not aware what kind of lighting the picture was taken in or the actual texture of the hair because most pictures are shot with filters and are tweaked and enhanced by technology, so it's nearly impossible to duplicate.

In real life, that blonde hair you see in the picture isn't really a pale silvery blonde highlight. It probably has tinges of yellow that were filtered out or photographed in intense natural light to appear lighter than it actually is. And in reality, that hair is probably a broken, dried-out mess. Try your best to educate them on the possibility of these untruths, pointing out the characteristics of what the picture shows and explain every detail carefully. This way, they understand that you are with them on this journey, but if necessary, you might need to detour a bit. If their vision is such, figure out a way for them to get real close, without causing any damage or despair. But remember to learn from what they are showing you. Pay attention to the details. They might not be able to get this exactly, but this is what they want.

I cannot count on both hands how many times a client has shown me a picture of soft spirally curls and asked me to perm their hair like that. No permanent wave will *ever* result in such a soft natural ripple. Perms are like Russian roulette. Hair wrapped tightly around a plastic rod held together with a rubber band, cured with acid, and stinks like rotten eggs—you are literally forcing straight hair to curl with chemicals, which is as unnatural as it gets. It already sounds like a recipe for disaster. And it never really works out well because anything you could've had in your body comes out in your hair, so it can cause an interference during chemical processes such as a permanent wave. If your client is on medication, recently had anesthesia, or even has her period, a perm doesn't take properly, resulting in frizzy, crimped-looking hair. Even if the gods were in your favor and all of the stars aligned, it still would never look like that perfect-picture head of curls. Anyone who lived through the '80s would agree. You hated your perm for the first month, and after a while, the smell lessened, it settled a bit, and it was tolerable. Unless you were blessed with naturally curly hair, no perm would ever get you close. The advice I give anyone who asks for one? Get yourself a curling iron or hot rollers, go on TikTok, and learn how to achieve the look that way.

Color-blind

Everyone's version of chestnut is completely different. I've gone to educational color classes, and we are asked to describe the hair color chestnut. To some, chestnut is a golden warm-brown tone, but to others, it's a cooler darker shade of brown. Almost every colorist in the class has a different version. The same issue can be said for Auburn. Some think vibrant ginger, where others debate that it is a brown with red undertones. And we are licensed professionals! Now ask a client. Good luck.

Clients say chestnut but show us drab, dark ash. They ask for Auburn, but if they see a speck of red, they'll freak out! They say they want caramel highlights, which we interpret as a darker golden tone, but the picture they show us is as pale as whipped butter. Balayage, biolage, Bellagio, potato, potahto—a client's interpretation and verbiage are always going to be different from ours, but it's our job to determine what they mean and execute what they want no matter how they say it.

Layer cake

"I only want two layers." That joke will never get old, still makes me laugh when I hear it. Do you mean you want two shelves added to your hair? There is no such thing as a numbered amount of layers. Layers are a scattering of lengths cut all around the exterior of the hair to add fullness or to the interior to decrease bulk and add texture. They are cut into the hair for various reasons and are intended to give either subtle movement or a defined, textured finish.

Imagine counting all your layers? There is no way to distinguish an actual amount, but thanks for the laugh. After a long day, sometimes we need that!

Science lab

Let's set the record straight. Permanent hair color will not harm your hair, especially professional-grade hair color that is offered at a salon. We know that it seems so dangerous to dip your toe in the pool of using permanent hair color, but if you want better gray coverage and for the color to last, you need it. Clients look absolutely terrified when we recommend using permanent hair color to achieve their goal, but if you are asking for something that requires coverage, lift, or change, semipermanent color or glaze will not do it. *Semipermanent* is exactly as it states: semipermanent. It only lasts for a short time, has little holding power, and will fade out after a few weeks of washing. Semipermanent color does not have enough strength to fully cover your grays, so it coats the strands instead, allowing for up to 50 percent gray coverage. There is no way to lighten your hair with semipermanent color. Simply put, it is a stain, and it has virtually no chemical backbone to open the cuticle to allow for lift.

Glaze, formerly known as toner, is similar concept to the glaze on a doughnut. It is a sheer outer finish meant to enhance or neutralize the current tone of your hair, a translucent coating that is meant to shine, correct, or slightly alter the tone of your existing color, which will fade after a few shampoos. It will not cover gray hair. It is recommended to visit the salon every few weeks to reglaze your hair, especially if you are looking to cancel brassiness from your blonde or to maintain the vibrancy of a red tone that is known to fade quickly.

Both versions are a great noncommittal way of entering the world of hair dye. Once you've joined the club and desire to make some changes, you will now have a better understanding of the science behind it and trust us to do what you need.

Here's a little science lesson in layman's terms: ammonia is an ingredient that is added to permanent hair dye. It is a necessary component that will safely crack open the shell of your strand to allow the color to seep in. I know ammonia sounds like a scary, triggering word, but it's *not* the ammonia you are thinking of, like the stinky, potent chemical your mom might've used to clean the bathroom. It is a safe and effective derivative that, through years of trial and error, has proven to be one of the only chemicals to allow the hair cuticle to open, accept the pigment, and safely close itself back up.

This scary rumor that hair color will damage your hair is completely false, especially if done by a licensed professional. Those misleading box dye kits? Now that shit is toxic. That's where the stigma comes from. One time using that box dye, you won't be able to comb your hair through for weeks. It's loaded with high concentrations of ammonia and other damaging substances that harden the hair, affecting the texture immediately. Even if it claims it is ammonia-free, trust me, it isn't. Like a fat-free cookie, they remove the fat but add in extra sugar and other toxic materials in place of it. Box dye companies remove the trigger word *ammonia* and replace it with ingredients equally as toxic that you cannot recognize, yet the consumer reads that it is free of ammonia, and they fall for it.

And they advertise it to look so easy. Of course this is a better option than going to a salon! And why, for the love of god, would you want to dye your own hair? What a mess! Your poor bathroom, you'll never get those stains out of the grout. You're not a trained professional, so why would you think you instantly become a colorist because you bought a box of hair dye? There are certain things you should always rely on a professional for. Ask yourself this: if your car broke down on the side of the road, would you lift the hood and try to fix it, or would you call AAA and let them handle it?

Stick to your day job. Leave your hair to a professional!

Guessing game

I believe that my inch and the client's inch are two different inches. They come in requesting two inches cut off of their length, and I measure it out with the ruler on my comb. I measure out the two inches that they requested, but in reality, it seems like four inches to them! They were envisioning more like a half an inch. Good thing I didn't just pick up those scissors and lob off those two inches because that would be one unhappy client with a way-too-short haircut! This is why communication is key. Visually show them, look at pictures, explain it all. Do not proceed until absolutely sure you are both on the same page.

What I have found to be most important before I dare to pick up my scissors or color brush to start is to repeat my plan verbally, even using my hands like a game of charades to show what I am about to do. Like someone giving directions, a client might say, "Right," but if you show them "right," they might realize they meant to say, "Left," like a scene from Laurel and Hardy, but in the end, neither one of us is laughing.

Perfect example: I'm giving my client a shaggy layered haircut, and I'm beginning to pivot the crown layers, so I simply ask which direction she wears the top. She begins to sing like Beyoncé, "To the left, to the left," so I did. I cut her hair to direct from the right side *to the left*. I get through the whole cut, blow her hair out, texturize for volume, add molding clay to make it full and piecey. And just as I'm about to pick up the can of hair spray to seal the deal, she says, "You know that I wear my hair directed the other way." She explains she *parts* her hair *on* the left over to the right.

So lesson learned: words can be confusing. Don't just say it, show it. It wasn't a total catastrophe. I altered her cut to go the opposite way. It was just a bit shorter than expected. And we renamed the song. We now both sing it together as "from the left, from the left!"

Working backward

One method that has always worked great for me when dealing with a client who cannot decide what they want: process of elimination. What *don't* you want?

- You don't want bangs? Great! No fringe for you.
- You don't want to see chunky highlights but want it lighter? Subtle babylight highlights it is.
- You don't want it to fall flat? Amazing! Layer the crown and texturize to remove weight to keep it voluminous.
- You need a ponytail? Length no shorter than the outer collarbone.

Works like a charm. Once you can decipher what a client does *not* want, you narrow it down until you come to some sort of conclusion. Like a card trick in a casino, you'll hit the jackpot every time.

This is why pictures, although misleading at times, are the best tool to figuring out what they really want. Use the pictures as a road map to find what they mean. An actual photo of where the length hits is a good indicator of how long or short they are talking about. The tone of that auburn color will tell how much red she will be able to handle. Is it bangs or just a higher peak of the face-framed angles that fall like a curtain-like bang without committing to an actual strong bang line? I could care less if a client brings in a ripped-out page from a magazine or has a Pinterest board of twenty-five different styles. A picture is worth a thousand words and will save your time and sanity to get to the bottom of what they want. You can take the length from one picture, the swept bangs of another, the multidimensional color of a different picture and create your own unique style geared to what will look best on the client. This isn't a store where you order style number 18, and *poof*, that's what you get. That's what make our jobs so unique. We are creating a one-of-a-kind masterpiece, bits and pieces from pictures but fine-tuned just for you.

Part-time critic

Everyone's a critic. Got a smartphone? You're practically one already. Opinions are like assholes; everybody's got one. But most of us were taught at an early age, if you have nothing nice to say, don't say it at all. I don't know why people feel their opinion about your business is so important that they need to go on social media to tell anyone who will listen. What credentials do they have? Are they connoisseurs of everything and the new authority on business management, or just a pain in the ass with a big ego and a Yelp account?

Some will review a business and leave rave reviews, trying to promote their favorite establishment, to tell others about the positive experience they received. But let's be honest. Those reviews are far and few between. Most people turn to this newfound self-appointed career to bash and complain because their experience was, in their opinion, not up to par with their standards, which clearly are pretty high. What they neglect to understand is how badly they can ruin a business with one click of their device. Their overrated opinion can put a hardworking business or service provider under scrutiny for all the world to see, directly affecting their reputation without any regard. Is it so necessary to tell the world that the chicken parmigiana was good, but the service was slow? Now anyone who reads that restaurant review will go into that restaurant with a negative feeling, assuming that their service will suck.

We've received great reviews on all avenues of social media, and yes, we've also received some unfavorable ones as well. We try very hard to make everyone happy, but regardless how hard you try, some people will always find fault. It's in their DNA; they are complainers by nature. There is nothing I or any of my employees wouldn't do to rectify a problem to make a client happier. If they verbalize it to us directly and explain to us in person, we will work together to make it all better. But to silently type in a poor review without bringing it to our attention? Coward, a keyboard renegade, tough and mighty at the keypad of their smartphone but weak and timid to our face. I'd have more respect if a client messaged me directly about a poor experience in my salon, respectfully bringing it to my attention without setting off any alarms for the world to see. But to sneak in a poor opinion of my business on a review? Shame on you.

Business owners do not have it easy these days. It doesn't matter if it's a hair salon, a restaurant, a doctor's offices, or even a gym. There will always be someone who likes to complain, and with modern technology, everyone is hearing their tales of woe in real time. Man, their hands must be tired from all of that typing. But my advice to them? Get a hobby. No one cares about your two cents.

So in walks a new client. She is an attractive Asian girl and has shoulder-length dark-brown hair. She was recommended by her coworker, a longtime client who has long, naturally blonde mermaid-looking hair, quite different from this new girl. Upon making her appointment, she asked for a few highlights, which doesn't require too much time at all.

As we began her initial consultation, she told me she wanted a full head of platinum-blonde highlights, which was a far more intricate process, requiring much more time that I had allotted, so I had to quickly rearrange my schedule to accommodate. As we started working, she began to bash the previous salon that she went to a year before, trying to achieve the same thing. I should've known I was walking into a land mine when she proudly told me that after being dissatisfied with her service at that other salon, she went on social media and gave them a terrible review. In her words, "that's what you do. It's a consumer's right to alert the public that a business isn't worth going to."

Immediately, I felt the hairs on my neck stand up, and I knew this might not end well, but because I was knee-deep into her process, it was already too late. What I realized halfway through was that her hair was not only naturally dark, she had colored the previous highlights over with box dye, which she neglected to tell me even though I asked during our consultation. Yada yada, the dark color wouldn't budge. Four hours later, and it was still brassy gold, and we were both frustrated to say the least. I explained to her that aside from having ethnic hair, the box dye was causing a block and would not let me lift it any lighter. There was no way I could push her hair any more than I did for fear it would break off. So after a deep conditioning treatment, we left off that we would give it a few weeks to relax and try to safely lift it again at another date.

Three days later, I was alerted to a scathing review on Yelp left by this girl that was so off the charts, I was speechless. Called me incompetent, said my salon was unprofessional, and worse than anything, referred to me as a racist because I said she had ethnic hair. Asian hair can be described as ethnic due to its strength and natural dark pigment and is known to be difficult to lighten, so in no way is that a racial comment or derogatory statement. I was merely stating a fact. She said I overcharged her and only came to me because her friend had beautiful blonde hair.

She vomited all over Yelp, telling the world what a bad experience she had, how she left in tears and was traumatized. Tears? She made a forwarding appointment and even tipped me! How traumatized could you be that you committed to another appointment to continue our journey? Not one word in that review of her secret home hair coloring session that caused her hair to stay stranded in an ugly brassy state, which was her fault not mine.

I called her on the phone, and she wouldn't answer. When I saw the coworker who recommended her, she said the girl never said a negative word to her and actually said although it couldn't be platinum, she liked it. WTF? I looked into her Yelp profile and was able to see every review she had ever posted, and—surprise, surprise—every one of them was negative. She even left a review for a Dunkin' Donuts, saying the doughnuts at that location were stale. I guess this is just another case of the keyboard renegade. Nothing better to do on a Friday night than spew out negativity just for kicks.

Bye, Felicia

I am a lot of things, but I am no quitter. I always give it 100 percent, and if someone is not satisfied, I work overtime to rectify it. But like Kenny Rogers sang, "you got to know when to hold them, know when to fold them, know when to walk away, know when to run." There are just some people who, no matter how hard you try, you will never truly make them happy. And you can't take it personally. These people are professional kvetchers. There is no restaurant, store, or service provider safe from their complaining. There will always be one piece in their haircut that feels uneven, one highlighted strand that seems brighter than the other, a shampoo assistant whom they do not want washing their hair, a bill that they think is too high.

This might sound crazy to some, but those are the clients I always seemed to attract. I strive on being that hairdresser who finally can make them happy. And believe it or not, I've succeeded many times. Nothing felt better than conquering these well-known toughies and making them smile. But perfect, I am not. With some, it was only a matter of time until I ran out of tricks and inevitably had to walk away.

What I have noticed lately is the newer generation of stylists are very quick to pull the trigger and fire a client the minute they hear a complaint. If they cause you anxiety, for any reason whatsoever, out they go. That is not how you do it. It is our job to accommodate them, and that means we are here by our choice to work to make them happy. And yes, it is very likely that they might not be, so it is our job to try…and sometimes try again. Just because a client complains or expresses unhappiness, that does not mean we walk away. It does not mean they are crazy and we have the right to refuse service. Take responsibility and do your best to figure out the problem and fix it. When and if you have exhausted all of your efforts and they are still not happy, than it might be time to pull the plug.

I've been around long enough to know the signs. It begins with a little nitpicking, then comes the doubtful body language in your chair, and when they finally leave, you are left feeling inept, wondering if they are happy or not. Eventually, the text messages begin, including poorly lit pictures taken in their bathroom showing you the issue they are having.

And with each complaint you pull through, gladly fixing what ails them, proving to them that their happiness is your number 1 priority. Until this just becomes the new normal, and every time they come in for an appointment, this routine is to be expected. It gnaws at you. You doubt yourself and your skills, and each time you see their name in your upcoming schedule, it puts a knot in your stomach. You keep muscling through each of their appointments, holding your breath until their kvetching begins again. Because as sure as the sun will rise the next day, they will have some little dilemma that needs immediate attention. Until you just can't take it anymore and you are going to explode.

But then something magical happens—the epiphany. You realize that you do not have to be a victim of this person's misery. You can refuse to service the client and move on with your life. Because their chronic nitpicking probably has nothing to do with you or their hair. It's about them. They have some other kind of drama happening in their life that they cannot control, so they take it out on the teeniest, tiniest detail, and in this case, it's their hair. And because they've paid you as a talented professional, it's your duty to comply.

You are allowing this to happen, and you can choose to shut the door and walk away. If this relationship becomes so toxic that it feels like a bad marriage and it stresses you out so much that you cannot do it for them another day, you can simply end ties and break up with a client. Set them free and let them find someone else to annoy.

Because one thing I learned to be true, if you gave every bit of your energy, expertise, and time to make them happy and they are still not, no one can.

You have one decision to make: stay in this abusive relationship or choose yourself. And when you do finally release them, it's feels like you gave birth, a freedom that you didn't know existed.

Save your energy for those who appreciate you. Your hard work should not go unnoticed. You have earned the trust and respect that you deserve. Truthfully, not every client and hairdresser will be a good fit, so if it's not clicking, that's okay. It leaves room in your schedule for someone who will be happy to be there.

Good Products And Hair Tricks

Standing behind a salon chair sometimes feels like I'm a teacher in front of a classroom. It is extremely important to educate our clients properly about correct product use and give them simple methods to style their hair. So often, clients return to us complaining that they were not able to duplicate the style they got on their the last visit. Anything new can be difficult to master, but if you don't arm your client with the tricks and tools they need to use, it's a recipe for failure, and they have you to blame.

We are artists, not salespeople. We don't sell; we create. As much as someone doesn't want to be given a sales pitch, trust me, it's more uncomfortable to give one. It's an awkward feeling when it comes off like we're just trying to sell products because that is definitely not the case. It has nothing to do with moving a product off of our retail shelf to make a sale. We are just trying to supply you with whatever you need to fix your problem, to get the job done right.

If you come in complaining that your hair is flat, and you wish you had more oomph, I'm going to pinpoint the best volumizing product to solve that, and I will demonstrate each detail on how to use said product. How much to dispense in your hands, when to put the product in, where to apply it, and where to avoid. I will ruin my own hairstyle and demonstrate on myself where to position the brush on the top of the head and show what angle to direct the blow-dryer to activate the product. I'll take every rabbit out of the hat to be sure you understand so you can do it right. That complimentary tutorial is part of my service because if you can duplicate at home and learn from my methods, I did my job. So when you leave our salon with your little bag of tricks armed with new products and all of my hairstyling secrets, I can rest easily, knowing you have everything you need.

But one thing is certain: you can't get that kind of passion from an online product description. And sadly, that's where most people wind up buying their products. I know Amazon has free delivery, and you can have it delivered in a day, blah, blah, blah, but it absolutely baffles me that in lieu of supporting your chosen stylist and their small business, you choose to buy it online or in a drugstore or retail chain. Our products are 100 percent authentic because they are shipped directly from the original manufacturer. Lord knows what third-party seller you are buying your products from when you decide to buy it elsewhere. Most of the time, those products are old and possibly expired, or a different product was added into the bottle to refill. And unless you know how the product should look, smell, or react like, you wind up with inauthentic crap for the same amount of money that you would've spent in our salon.

We do cartwheels demonstrating all of our tricks with a product, trying so hard to fix the issue you brought to our attention, and we catch you snap a picture of the bottle and find out you bought it elsewhere. We are putting in all of that effort to try to do what is right for you. All we ask is for your trust and your support of our business. Small businesses are slowly being pushed out of contention by big corporations that are not even licensed to sell these particular products. Yet they do, and you take the bait.

When we recommend products to you, it's like a doctor prescribing medication. We understand your hair and what your hair goals might be. We are diagnosing your issue and prescribing the antidote to your dreams. We are trained to troubleshoot your hair dilemmas, by understanding what you have and what you want. As a relatable example, I was told that almost every woman wears the wrong-sized bra. We all think we know what a good fit is for us until an expert shows us differently. I didn't believe it at first until I got professionally fit by a corsetiere, and to my surprise, I had been completely wrong all of these years. I, too, thought I knew what my size was, but a professional taught me what I needed. And once I followed her advice, I realized the professional was right, and my "girls" have never looked better!

If we left you to your own devices and didn't work to help you understand your hair issues, you'd become so jaded by the misleading advertisements that are everywhere and purchase things that will not help you. Let's say, for example, you have fine-textured hair and think you have frizz, but in reality, you might not be blowing your hair properly, so it looks out of whack, leading you to believe you might need frizz-fighting products to smooth it out. While strolling down the aisle at CVS, coupon in hand, you stop in front of the antifrizz products to find yourself the perfect remedy.

What you are not aware of is majority of those products contain waxes, silicone, and oil, which would be too overwhelming for your fine hair, but since you diagnosed yourself, *and* the pretty-looking bottle promises it'll do the trick, it must be true. And it smells great, like the scent of a tropical vacation, so of course it's going to be a winner. Not sure how much to use, you squeeze out a heaping dose of product, blob it on your hair and hope for the best. What you were left with is just another bottle of crappy product that didn't work to add to the beauty product graveyard under your bathroom sink. Your hair is greasy, weighed down with residue, and because your original problem wasn't frizz at all, you just weren't blowing your hair correctly, it's still frizzy. It might even be a reputable professional product that you purchased to try, but if your trusted professional hair guru didn't recommend it or explain to you how to use it, it's already a fail.

I believe that there is a who, what, when, where, why, how to product use. Let me explain:

Who is the client in question? Because everyone has different hair, and not every head with the same style are treated or handled equally. Some heads need different types of product to achieve the same look as another head.

What is the problem you're trying to fix? What type of finish are you hoping to achieve or problem to solve?

When is the correct time to add each product? You might need a few products to achieve your style, but not all products are applied at the same time. For example:

- Leave-in conditioner or heat-protectant serum is applied when the hair is wet while your cuticle is open to allow the product to sink deep into the strand for the best protection. That will help to add moisture and gently seal the cuticle to prime the hair for heat styling. If it was applied to your dry hair, it can leave a greasy finish by sitting on the outside of the cuticle and would not provide any protection from dangerous thermal heat.
- Volumizing products like root lifters, thickening gels, or mousse are usually applied when the hair is still damp because they are heat activated to deliver maximum volume. Products like that are wet-hair products. You should not apply them to dry hair because they will feel sticky and not be effective.
- Molding paste or pomade should be used on dry hair because if you are trying to achieve a wispy or piecey look, it will not adhere to hair when water is present. So it is saved until the hair is dry and ready to be finished. Those types of products provide texture and movement to complete your style.
- Hairspray is generally used as a finisher, so for obvious reasons, it's mostly used when your style is complete. However, hair spray is essential when sprayed on the hair before you add curls with an iron. It acts as a starch, giving more support and hold so your curls will last longer.

Where does the product get applied and *why*?

- Root lifter goes exactly where it states—the roots! These types of products contain hydrolyzed starch meant to increase volume, which starts at the root. If a product like that is applied incorrectly to the ends instead, it will add stiffness to the ends, making it difficult to style and add unnecessary weight, causing the hair to lay heavy.

- Smoothing serum or protective oil should be applied to the midshaft and the ends of the hair, not at the roots. Otherwise, you run the risk of oiliness in the scalp area. These products are necessary to help give protection from heat tools, and the most vulnerable areas to be traumatized from heat are mostly our ends.

- Focus on shampooing your roots then conditioning your ends. All too often, clients focus shampoo toward the ends and avoid the scalp, neglecting the removal of natural scalp oils, product buildup, sweat, and dry skin. Then they slop on conditioner to the root area, making it greasy while it should be distributed to the ends or ponytail first for proper detangling.

How can be how much, how often? How big of a brush is needed? How do I create volume? How do I make the hair shiny and smooth? How do I stop flyaways? The list goes on and on.

It's like a master's degree in hairstyling. Some of it is so easy and requires just simple common sense, yet clients assume there must be a hundred moves and angles and tools to execute a style. I teach them steps to break it down, to help make their styling efforts easier. How to start from point A and confidently get themselves to point B using the tips and tricks I've taught them. When they watch me demonstrate on my own head, it gives the client visual insight as to brush placement, my hand position, direction of the blow-dryer, or how much product to scoop out or spray. These tips are worth their weight in gold and is what keeps us different from any other operator.

Many other stylists silently do their job, and the client sits in the chair like a mannequin, not sure what is going on or what products are being used. They are not offered any tips to duplicate the style at home. My clients know the difference. At my salon, they learn from us because we care. I could give them the greatest new style, but if they can't understand how to work with it and style it properly at home, it's a bad style. My clients go home filled with great knowledge, knowing that I've worked diligently to make them understand. And if they can handle the new look and style it with ease, I did my job.

Some clients seem to have amnesia and cannot remember the dissertation of rules we verbally gave them while executing their style in the chair that day. But after a few weeks of frustrated styling, their problem becomes our problem. We need to remember that they are walking billboards and social media critics of our work, so we do what is right to fix the issue and reeducate them again.

Regardless of the gripe, an unhappy client is a terrible advertisement. At the end of the day, it is our responsibility to help rectify any unhappiness. Give a little, get a lot. Keep them happy even if you know it's not your fault. If you show that you care, they will eventually listen. Your name is on it, as is your reputation. Nothing makes a client feel heard like the helpful response from their trusty hairdresser. I realized this a long time ago: if they feel important, they will always come back.

Every so often, clients leave our salon ecstatic, so in love with their hair, but will reach out a few weeks later expressing frustration. Their color faded, or their hair seems dried out from the excessive heat styling that could be required for this new chosen look. It could be so many reasons why, and we work to help troubleshoot the issue. We never let a client leave without properly educating them as to the correct home care.

- Do not use excessively hot water when you wash your hair. Aside from drying out your scalp and hair, hot water will open the cuticle, and aside from drying your hair out, there goes your color down the drain. Warm water, not hot, is the correct temperature to cleanse your hair. We do not care what you do to your body with hot water from the neck down. It's the neck up that we are responsible for, so stop steaming up those mirrors and turn that water to warm when it's needed for your hair!
- That does not mean we want you to wash with cold water, either. Cold water is not the appropriate temperature to use when washing your hair because it cannot activate the enzymes in the shampoo. It actually congeals the product

and won't allow it to lather, hence not properly cleansing your hair. But if you choose, when shampooing and conditioning is complete, cold water is perfect for a final rinse to seal the hair cuticle and add shine.

- Brush your hair thoroughly before getting into the shower or bath. Removing your hair of any tangles will help avoid a matted mess once the water hits it. You will also help to release tough product buildup to allow for a more effective wash. Otherwise, the water hits that shellacked hair helmet, and it turns to a gluey mess.

- Do not wash your hair every day. Skip a day or two because excessive washing will strip your hair color and dry out your tresses. You need those essential scalp oils that naturally occur to keep your scalp healthy, which in turn promotes proper hair growth. Try brushing your hair every day to pull those healthy oils through the strands, making the scalp feel less oily and nourishing the rest of the hair. Your hair and scalp will thank you.

- Make sure your hair clean is before coming to your color appointment. I know your grandma always told you in order to get your hair colored, the dirtier it was, the better. That was back in the old days when hair color contained such high levels of toxic chemicals, and all that product buildup or natural oils acted as a buffer to protect your scalp and hair from irritation. Professional hair color products of today are much more gentle than they used to be, so there is less chance of experiencing a chemical reaction or irritation. In order to get the maximum benefit of your color service, your hair should be rid of product buildup and excessive oil and free of perspiration. Having your hair clean provides a good canvas for your color to take properly. Here are reasons why:

  ○ If your hair has a buildup of product, the color will cling to the product, and as the product begins to break down, so will your color.

- Excessive oil on the scalp can actually repel the color from absorbing into the strands, therefore resulting in poor gray coverage and improper lift.
- Sweat contains your own natural salt, and when traces of former perspiration are present in the hair during your color service, it changes the porosity and can cause your color to take too dark.

- Wait at least twenty-four hours to wash your hair *after* receiving a color service. You need to allow the cuticle some time to naturally seal itself closed in order to hold your color properly.
- Use recommended shampoo and conditioner—recommended by us, not Pantene, or some crap you bought at target. I don't care that it sounds French, TRESsemé (and all things next to it in the same beauty aisle in CVS) is terrible for your hair, and we cannot guarantee that your hair will hold up if you use crappy store-bought products. Drugstore-brand shampoos contain detergent, which is why they lather so well and smell so great. Most of them have a PH balance equivalent to Dawn dishwashing liquid, and yes, it will get your hair squeaky clean—but a little too clean, stripped of all the natural oils that are meant to protect your scalp and strands, making it extremely porous and dry. Also, using other types of over-the-counter products will cause hair to become built up with all of the wax and filler that are used to make that crap. Because yes, crap it is.
- While in the shower, brush your conditioner through with a detangling brush before rinsing. It helps to evenly distribute a smaller amount of conditioner, lubricating each strand while brushing. Always start from the bottom of your hair, working your way higher as you go to avoid causing a traffic jam of knots. Doing this ritual will eliminate excessive shedding because it's a safer and more effective way to detangle than using your hands. When it's time to rinse,

start rinsing from the front hairline, brushing through to help remove excess traces of conditioner so your rinsing and detangling is efficiently done.

- Keep your hair protected from heat tools. The fabric of your hair is as delicate as a silk blouse. As you would with a silk garment, your hair must be treated gently; otherwise, you will ruin it. You must use a good thermal protector before heat styling; otherwise, it will look dry and potentially frizzle off. You need to put a buffer between your delicate hair and the intense heat of styling tools. Nothing is as damaging to hair as 450 degrees of heat sandwiching your hair while flat ironing or forced hot blow-dryer air blowing directly at your fragile tresses. A barrier wall of heat protectant will fend off some of the damage caused by these necessary heat tools. You don't cook chicken in a pan unless you coat the surface with oil or butter. It'll stick to the bottom and burn. Use that analogy when dealing with your hair. Apply a good styling product or heat protectant to guard it from scorching, just like that poor burnt chicken.

- Apply your styling products in doses. Imagine you spill out a palm full of product and try to apply it all to one part of your hair. All that excess product drips through your fingers. Your hair becomes too greasy and overwhelmed with too much goop. Use smaller amounts and distribute through sections of your hair, going back for more for the next section. You will use less product and focus on smaller areas to properly apply. More is not better; more is just waste.

- Hair spray should be sprayed on your hair from a distance and land on your hair as a dry invisible shield, not a coat of armor. The first three to five inches of any spray are mostly propellant, so at close range, it will leave a wet residue on your hair, resulting in a hardened finish. I advise my clients to spray their hair using a ninety-degree angle from their arm, about eight to ten inches from your head. This way, the spray is dry by the time it lands on your hair. It will have the same great hold but be more touchable and natural feeling.

- PSA: clean out the lint trap of your blow-dryer with flames coming out of it! The air flows from the vented area through the dryer onto your hair. Like any mechanical system, there's an intake and an outtake. If it's clogged with dust, the air cannot circulate, causing the blow-dryer air to heat up unnecessarily, turning your blow-dryer into a blowtorch! Take a dry toothbrush and clean out the screen and any built-up dust on a regular basis. It will increase the life span of your dryer and save your hair from scorching.

- Replace your brushes after a few months. If the bristles on your brush are no longer straight and seem hooked over and melted shorter, it's time for a new brush. The excessive heat needed to blow-dry your style will wear down the bristles over time. Your strands will get caught up in the hook and rip during your styling sessions, causing breakage and unrepairable damage.

- Protect your hair from the sun, chlorine, and salt water. Harmful rays alone, or along with pool and ocean water, causes hair to radically break down. The texture becomes weak and frizzy, hair color gets brassy and oxidized, and the strands become dry and tangled, making necessary brushing nearly impossible. We are not saying to avoid a potentially beautiful beach day. Just be prepared.

  This is the sun advice I give to all of my clients, and I personally follow these rules as well:

  o Before heading out for your day in the sun, wet your hair thoroughly in the shower.

  o Apply conditioner to your hair and do not rinse out. Leaving a film of conditioner on your hair will act as a barrier wall, shielding your strands from the sun's harmful rays. It works as a conditioning treatment, allowing the sun to bake the conditioner into your hair, promoting softness and color retention. Hair is very porous material. It will easily soak in salty or chemically altered water. If your wet hair is coated with conditioner, it will take a long time for the water to break it down and harm your hair.

- o Once you are done swimming, it is important to rinse your hair with clean water and reapply more conditioner to keep it well protected. There's always a shower available at a beach or pool facility. And if not, simply using your bottle of drinking water will do the trick. It is necessary to rinse because if your hair air dries with the salt or chlorinated water on top of the strand, it will dissolve its top layer, causing damage and oxidation. Reconditioning after a postswim rinse will ensure you are supplying your hair with enough moisture to keep everything intact and healthy.

- o Speaking of sun, hair extensions are known to react badly to sunscreen and excessive sun exposure. Some sunscreens contain octocrylene and avobenzone (butyl methoxydibenzoylmethane). While necessary for good skin protection, it can cause a chemical reaction on light-colored extensions. We've seen blonde extensions turn pinkish orange from the slightest bit of sunscreen, so be careful when applying sunscreen to tie up and cover your very expensive extensions. That tinge of color is impossible to remove once it's present, resulting in having to purchase new hair extensions. That's one expensive day at the beach!

- o Bleached hair is subject to this discoloration as well and will require many corrective color processes to fix. It's best to follow the rules in the previous paragraph. Wet your hair with clean water and coat with conditioner for a day at the beach to be safe. Being blonde is an investment, so a lot of effort on your part is needed to avoid a problem. It seems exhausting to be blonde! I guess they really don't have as much fun after all.

- Rebook and stay on schedule to maintain your look. Maintenance is key. Your color will oxidize in a few weeks, so it will need to be freshened up. Your haircut will grow in four to six weeks, and all the lines of your cut will be in need of a trim. Those extensions will gap and need a readjustment. After a few weeks of regrowth, those pesky roots will reappear, needing to be touched up. If you let it spiral out of control and are not taking proper care of your hair as well, it's a recipe for disaster.

I believe having great hair is 50 percent what I did in the salon and 50 percent what you are doing at home. We are a partnership, and it requires your participation to stay on track. And please consider rebooking before you leave because nobody respects a beggar.

If you are happy, scream it from the rooftops. The best advertisement is a referral from a happy customer. We are always willing to welcome new clients to our chair. It speaks volumes that you are so pleased with our work, you want to share with your nearest and dearest. Write us a nice review on social media and be our walking billboards. We planted the seeds and love to watch it grow.

So much common sense and knowledge go into what I do behind the chair. We're not just a pretty face with a pair of shiny new scissors. Part of our job is to be a wealth of information, and I'm happy to share all that I know to keep you looking so great. Our guidance needs to go home with you so you can understand why things happen and how to avoid it in the future. And if you are not learning it from your chosen stylist, then you are definitely in the wrong chair.

PTSD

Walking down this path of reflection as I wrote this book has been very cathartic, and I'm amazed to think how far I have come, and a twinge of pride makes me realize how successful a path this has been.

But along this journey, it has unleashed many memories of things I've locked away and never really took the time to focus on. I've come to the realization that many of the experiences that I went through to get to where I am today were pretty toxic, and I am experiencing an overwhelming case of PTSD as I relive them all over again, putting it all down on paper.

We grow from our past experiences, and what we do from that point on is our choice. We can either follow in suit and take it on as our behavior or make a conscious effort every day to do it differently, to rise above and follow a more positive path. I have always believed that struggle is a very good motivator because when you feel like the chips are down, you have no one but yourself to get you out of it. You can wish upon every star in the sky or pray for a genie in a bottle to get you to a better place, but realistically, no one can make your life better but you. There's no sugar daddy to swoop in and give you the life of your dreams. You need to put on your big-girl/boy bloomers and figure it out for yourself. You're broke? Get busy working and save your money. In a bad relationship? Ditch that anchor and sail on to a better life. Not busy behind the chair? Start promoting your work and getting your name out there. And all of that I did. But along with all of those life decisions, I've had to rise above a lot of negativity that was put on me by others who were using me for their own personal gain or pleasure.

Coworker

In my first job, I worked closely with a stylist who had a very intimidating personality, who tried every way she could to stifle my growth up the ladder. When I was an assistant, she would monopolize my help away from the other stylists and bully me to do whatever she wanted. She was nice on the surface but would turn on me on a dime. For instance, she would have me sneak and fill up all of her personal product bottles from the refill gallons at the salon when the boss wasn't around yet ratted me out to him the one time I filled up a little shampoo in mine.

As I grew into a stylist, the behavior became more intense, and I had to work very hard to tune it out and stay on my path. She would try to build alliances with the other stylists to talk about what I wore or the work that I did. It was worse at the time of my career while I was trying to transition from an assistant to a stylist. If I had a new client in my chair and I was trying my best to act professionally and poised as if I had been doing this for years, she would choose that moment to tell me out loud in front of my customer that her client was due in soon, and I should wash them for her when I was done.

Another time, I asked her advice on a color formulation, one that was similar to a color that she had just done for one of her own clients. Little did I know, she *Marie Baroned* me by sabotaging the formula, telling me to use all of the wrong colors, resulting in the client being very unsatisfied. She then swooped in and stole the client, telling her that I was new and less experienced and promised that she could fix it.

Always taking every opportunity to make me look or feel inadequate just for her own personal satisfaction. Always in competition, always afraid I would steal her customers or do better than she did. I knew even back then that it was toxic behavior, but I just thought that was the way it was. I have never been the type to think people would be jealous of me or of anyone else's life or career, but it is clear, looking back now, that she was envious and intimidated of my growth.

Knowing that I was able to grow as I did in spite of her is remarkable. Maybe this kind of battle was healthy after all. It fueled me to work hard and prove that I could be better. And at this point, it has become a classic case of the student becoming the master. While she is still working in that very same salon and never grew, I moved on and exceeded her on many levels.

We periodically keep in touch, but she remains guarded when we talk shop. And I've owned my salon for eighteen years, very near to where she lives and works, and not once has she ever come to visit. I guess if she doesn't see it with her own eyes, it doesn't exist, and she wins.

Friend or foe

When I left where I was working to open my own salon, I brought along a good work friend of mine whom I hired to become my desk manager. I trusted her judgment and appreciated her help during those shaky first few years. As time went on, I started to feel her become more negative and distant toward me, and I tried to give her space and find ways to make her happy. I hired an additional desk receptionist to help ease her workload and paid her for days that she had to tend to some personal family issues.

I began to notice that my schedule hadn't been accommodating clients late into the evening the way I used to, and I questioned her as to why that was. She shrugged and said that no one requested late appointments. A few weeks later, I ran into a client whom I hadn't seen in a few months, and she apologized that she had to start going to another salon because I wasn't available late evenings to accommodate her anymore like I used to be. Little did I know, my manager was purposely not making those appointments because *she* did not want to stay late. When I brought this to her attention, she proceeded to chastise me, telling me that not all salons are open late like we were and that if the clients really wanted to be serviced by me, they would leave work early and come during normal work hours.

She approached my clients for personal favors without ever getting my permission and started to use my appointments as leverage, asking the clients to help her out with something she might've needed, and she would put them to the top of the wait list. I had no idea that was going on until she propositioned one of my police officer clients, bargaining his hair appointment for a desired PBA card, and he was so offended that he brought it to my attention.

She also started to tell me that my staff was unhappy and uncomfortable around me, that I had to stop micromanaging everyone; otherwise, they were all going to leave. Shocked and sad that my so-called behavior was affecting everyone so badly, I became passive and kept quiet when I really wanted to run my business the way I intended. What I found out later was she operated like a double agent, trying to turn some of my employees against me to mold me into the pushover that she wanted me to be.

I put up with her moodiness and negativity for a while, figuring if I did it her way it would all be better. But unfortunately, I created a monster, and these were now the new rules, and out of nowhere, I had a silent business partner. Her behavior was out of control, and the tables needed to be turned back to where they belonged. It was a tough breakup because aside from affecting my business and causing me to have to reconfigure my management team, I also lost a friend. I realize now that I had lost her long before that, but the finalization of it all hurt like a knife.

But now looking back and reliving it again as I write this life journal, I am so ashamed of myself that I let someone get in the way of my journey. How dare I allow her to have such authority when this whole venture rides on me? I invested every dime I had and every ounce of my soul into this business, and I allowed her to possibly derail my dream.

After that day, I never allowed anyone to get in my way. I will not apologize for how I run my business because I do it professionally and with respect and integrity toward both my clients and my staff. If an employee cannot or will not work to stay on this ship, then they have to get off the next port.

Clients

Through my career, I have had clients make me feel inadequate. Some would consistently reference their former stylist, singing their praises, and always find something to nitpick about my work at the end of their service. As you could imagine, the sleepless nights and heightened insecurity it caused was boundless. I reached my boiling point with one specific client. I just couldn't take it anymore. I blatantly asked the client why she doesn't go to that stylist anymore being that my work was subpar in comparison. I muscled up enough courage to tell her that I didn't think we were a good match to keep her as a client anymore. If her former hairdresser was so amazing, she should return to them. I realized in that moment that you can't make everybody happy, and keeping them in your chair is like committing a dangerous form of self-sabotage. Set them free and move on to people who will appreciate your work and value your commitment to them.

I found out years later that she did the same routine to another hairdresser about me. Raved about me and all of my talent, making that hairdresser also feel inadequate. I guess it wasn't me after all. This is just how she is. And you can't teach an old dog new tricks.

Authenticity is key

I was an assistant at a different salon for a few weeks when I was sixteen. I was assisting the colorist one day and sat in on her consultation with the client. She was upselling this new Italian color line, which was an up charge from the Clairol crap that they usually offered. She explained all of the benefits of having her use this more-expensive product on her hair, and the client agreed to upgrade her service.

During her service, I saw her applying the Clairol color out of the squeeze bottle to the client's head, not using the brush application of the fancy Italian product. Little did I know, it was just a sales pitch for a higher ticket, and the colorist never intended on using it in the first place.

Confused, I outed her by asking the client if she changed her mind about choosing the more-expensive color, being that the colorist was using the traditional crap. The angry colorist took me into the back room and scolded me for not keeping my mouth shut. She would never let me assist her again and was mean to me whenever we worked together. She hid behind her dishonesty by telling the rest of the staff that I was a terrible assistant and that I couldn't be trusted.

I hung in for only a few more weeks, but I had no choice but to leave. It was through that situation that I realized that in order to be truly authentic as a stylist, you have to be authentic as a person.

First job

My very first job was in a neighborhood salon up the street from my school. I was fifteen when I started, so I had no clue as to how anything worked as an employee of a salon. It was a tight-knit family-run operation, and I trusted if the other employees weren't complaining about things, why should I?

As an assistant, we were paid a flat day rate, which was far below minimum wage, but I was told that was normal because we earned tips as well. When I would ask for a raise or questioned the salary, I was gaslit and told that I got compensated in education, that I was learning a skill every day on the job, so you couldn't put a price on that luxury. Not sure what kind of education I could learn by cleaning the salon top to bottom, but it apparently has helped me keep my salon extremely neat till this day.

Being an assistant branching into a stylist was a tough time because I was starting to work behind the chair as a hairdresser yet still had to clean and maintain the function of the salon as an assistant. As I began to service paying clients, I expected to be compensated with a little commission for the money I was bringing into the salon. Payday would come, and I'd receive a salary of my usual assistant day rate, no extra money to compensate any extra that I brought in behind the chair. I asked why, and I was told that I wasn't eligible yet for commission because I was still in training. Once my work behind the chair was more consistent and my tickets doubled my weekly salary, I would get half of everything over that amount, which only calculates to a few buck over my regular pay. I was doing two different jobs and still only being paid for one.

When I expressed my frustration, I was shamed and gaslit again. Told I was being selfish and wasn't a team player and was only concerned about money. Shamed for having so much effort given to me to grow and that I was acting unappreciative. Told if I really wanted to grow, I had to work my ass off every day to accommodate clients with no questions asked. I was working six days a week at that point and was expected to come in many times to take care of a client on my one day off. I was eighteen or nineteen, so I was naive enough to believe that, so I retracted my anger and continued on.

When I finally graduated to a full-time stylist, my bookings grew, and my career began to take off. I became one of the top earners among the rest of the stylists, making 50 percent of whatever I booked. But I would receive my paycheck and notice that a certain amount would be additionally deducted from my salary each week, and I had no idea why that was. I showed it to my accountant, and he explained to me that the amount that was being taken from my pay was actually the amount of FICA that was required to be paid by the boss.

I brought this to the salon owner's attention and again was met with another round of gaslighting. Even though I was paid as a W-2 employee, I was told I was considered an independent contractor, that I made my own hours and ran my own business in the salon, and the 50 percent portion that the business received was equivalent to paying rent. I knew that was highly unethical and also illegal. That reality helped me make the decision that it was time to move on.

I never believed a day rate was fair, so moving forward, I have never paid any of my employees anything less that an hourly rate. If you got paid fifty dollars a day and one day you worked five hours, it was around ten dollars per hour. But if the next day you worked ten-plus hours, that's less than five dollars per hour, so it never computed to anything fair.

I did learn a lot from that experience, and I realize now that I buried it away very deep in my soul. I'm angered and frustrated that

I carried on believing this was the way and feel foolish that I let it happen. I do know that he always had my best interest at heart but only as long as it benefited him first. He did genuinely care about my education and was proud of the work I did, but I am aware that my success contributed to his success, as it does in every business where individuals make money to keep the company thriving.

Venturing into my own business, I do everything I can to be honest and accountable with both my staff and my clients, knowing I wouldn't be able to look at myself in the mirror if I took advantage of them in any way. I named my salon Karma for many reasons, and this was definitely one of them.

Nailed

In the beginning years of owning my salon, we used to offer nail services in a small department in my space. It was a nice extra accommodation for clients to have a one-stop-shop type of experience so they could get their nails done while their color processed or before/after their hair appointment to save a trip elsewhere. It worked out great for a long time, and although it was an entity that I did not know much about, I had skilled operators who did, and it brought in a lot of extra business.

My nail technicians did not rent space from me to do their business. They were employees of my salon. I funded all things needed to run that department, and my desk staff took care of all of their bookings and transactions as they did for my hair department.

This particular nail technician did amazing work and could execute a lengthy nail service in record time. She was in high demand and was fully booked out for weeks at a time. But skilled or not, she always seemed to defy salon protocols and make up her own rules as if she owned the joint. I found myself butting heads with her on multiple occasions. She was the only employee I ever had who took every opportunity to bend my rules in her favor even after I told her no. She would "Jedi mind trick" me by trying to convince me that it wasn't going to be a problem when it was *clearly* going against my business practice, and it would be.

If she decided to make social plans at the end of the workday or plan a last-minute vacation, of course without running it by me first, she would order my desk staff to move her appointments around at the last minute or harass the clients to move to a different day or to an earlier inconvenient time to accommodate her personal agenda. I discussed with her many times that clients schedule their appointments to accommodate *their* needs and that it was not fair or professional to ask them to leave work or family responsibilities to accommodate our personal life.

When my desk staff knew it was going against my rules and would refuse her request, she would go behind my back and text them from her own phone. Many clients had conferenced me privately to complain about this and would inevitably leave and get their nail services elsewhere.

She did whatever she wanted. Whether it was arriving late to work, rearranging her schedule to suit her own needs, or decide to color her hair in the middle of the workday, twenty minutes before her client was due, the word *no* didn't seem to compute in her head. Her defiance was a common occurrence and a slap in my face to my business practice. This type of unprofessional behavior undermined my authority as the boss and affected the culture of my salon, making my other employees feel like they could bend the rules too.

One particular day, I finally reached my boiling point. The hair department was insanely busy, and our two assistants were occupied, helping us accommodate the overflow of clients. Obviously ignorant to what was going on around her, she asked if one of the assistants could apply her hair color because she was done for the day. I told her no and explained that they were too busy helping us with our clients. As a courtesy, I always allowed my staff to use my hair color, but it had to be done when the time was appropriate, and this clearly wasn't the time. Bells are chiming, colors need to be washed off, and now one of my assistants is nowhere to be found.

After calling her name for the third time with no response, I stopped servicing my client to see where she was. Oh, I found her, hiding in the back room, applying this nail technician's hair color. Like the pied piper, the nail tech had a way of dominating my assistants to do what she needed. She completely disregarded me and took advantage even after I told her no. I've got a salon full of clients who need to be washed and attended to, but like her usual antics, she did what she wanted. Caught like deer in the headlights, they both saw the steam coming out of my ears and knew they were in trouble. My assistant immediately stopped and ran out to wash the client as this one began to explain that I was overreacting and that it wasn't a big deal.

I've had a few aha moments in my life when the light bulb goes on, and everything seems very clear. Regardless how busy an operator she was or how much money she made for the salon, it was not worth the aggravation to deal with this behavior any further. She was the perpetual rock in my shoe, and it was time to take that shoe off, shake it out, and move on. It was always going to be something with her, and this was just an example of how my life was with her in it. If it wasn't one thing, it was always going to be another.

As the owner of this business, it's my right to place rules and protocols for all of my staff to abide by. The blatant disregard for my authority was not going to be tolerated, and the money she generated for my salon was not going to be the thing I cave over to keep me going. It was better to cut it free and have less stress to carry on. I made a decision that day to let her go, and I never looked back.

Workhorse

I was trained from the very beginning to make work my number one priority. I felt the only way to grow in this career path was to hustle, and I needed to stay behind that chair to make it happen. I was guided not to pay attention to opportunities and social events that came my way that would have caused me to take a break from work because I had to keep my eye on the prize. I was convinced I was on the right path, and I must admit that the effort it took definitely paid off and got me to the level of success I dreamed of. But it came with a lot of fine print.

Sixty to sixty-five hours a week in a salon, standing on my feet, with no freedom or much free time. I hardly ever took a lunch hour or any break during the day at all. Although I had a life outside the salon, it was navigated and worked around my job. Looking back now, I have no idea why I did it. I get angry at myself thinking how much of my youth was so focused and work-driven, and realize only now what a mistake that might've been. Work was everything. I actually used to cut out of class in high school not to goof off with my friends but to go to work to take care of clients who could only come during the day! I look back in regret that I didn't really get to enjoy myself more or take the time to find a work/life balance. Only now, with so much focus on this mantra of "work smarter, not harder" do I realize what a fool I was to be so work-driven.

Don't get me wrong, I do not regret my career or the choices I've made to get here, but Jesus Christ, what would've been the big deal if I took an indulgent weekend off every now and again? Leave early to meet up with friends at happy hour? Take two weeks off at any time of the year that I wanted to really chill and explore an unknown location to see what the world was like somewhere else instead of cramming it all into a five-day vacation scheduled around the busy salon seasons, to a moderate location that I would be sure to get back as soon as I could for work. Every vacation I took, I'd work late on a Saturday, with barely enough time to get ready to fly off early Sunday morning, just to be back to work by the following weekend. It was like I was a machine, and I realized I robotically functioned for most of my life, and sadly I still do. I'm trying very hard to take the opportunities to sneak away for a weekend with friends, or just take off for a mental health day, but after all of these years functioning like this, it has me feeling guilty about it. Now that I'm learning to correct it, I am disappointed that I lost so much of that valuable time, and that it took me this long to understand it.

This wasn't a fun stroll down memory lane, and for good reason, I learned to compartmentalize these situations and pack them away so as not to relive them. I understand now that these situations were pivotal to my success, sand as hard or degrading as they were to experience, they were just strategies others used to deter my growth for their personal gain. And I didn't let them. But the only way to the other side is going through it one last time before you finally put it out with the trash for good.

They say going to the hairdresser is like paying a visit to your therapist or hanging with a bartender. Usually it's business as usual, casual chitchat and a pleasant service. But sometimes it's like an episode of *Punk'd* because unless you were there, you wouldn't believe it was true.

Through the years, I've experienced some head-shaking antics that took place in the salon. Just like the craziness that occurs during a full moon cycle, we get a front-row seat to some unbelievable situations. As a professional, it's my responsibility to diffuse drama and keep everyone else present unaware of the nonsense in the moment, but sometimes I am stunned with my jaw on the ground, just like everyone else in the room!

Five-finger discount

A client came in for a scheduled highlight-color service, as she did many times in the past. She had just had a baby and was happy to spend a few hours away from her kids getting serviced at our salon. As I walked to the couch to greet her, I noticed a bottle of detangling spray from our retail shelf right next to her purse. As I moved her over to the color station and got her draped for her color service, I realized that the bottle of spray was missing. She didn't bring it over to the color area, nor was it left on the couch, back on our retail shelf, or placed at the front desk for later at checkout.

I casually inquired about the whereabouts of the product to the client and to my desk manager, and the client seemed confused as to what product I was referring to, saying she didn't have it. She quickly changed the topic, passionately discussing her new favorite TV series in an apparent attempt to distract me from the missing bottle.

As I began her color service, I mentioned the mystery of the missing product once again, and she acted like she had no idea what I was talking about. I know it's a product that she uses, and I clearly saw it sitting next to her in the couch. The inventory count was off, and my desk manager agreed that she saw her remove it from the shelf as she arrived, and now it was MIA.

As time passed, my suspicion grew, and I was now convinced she took it. She was extremely territorial about her handbag, and without directly asking her to look in there, I again mentioned the whereabouts of the missing bottle, giving her an opportunity to open it up and act surprised that she "might've" accidentally placed it in there without thinking. Still nothing.

We complete the color service and head up to the reception area for her to check out and pay. I am literally sweating, knowing she is going to walk out getting away with stealing a stupid twenty-eight-dollar product, so I boldly ask her to please check her bag for the missing item. She hesitates, unzips the bag, and ta-da! There it was, right where I knew it was the whole time!

She casually places it on the desk and says, "Oh, and I'll take this too"

Of course you were, but now you'll actually have to pay for it! I was so flabbergasted and at a loss for words that I just walked away from the desk. She paid her bill, even lingered to set up a following appointment, and left like nothing happened. We are all completely dumbfounded as to the gall on this girl.

Clearly, with a salon named Karma, I will not tolerate any form of dishonesty in my salon. I reach out to her on the phone in an effort to break up with her. I explain that due to the situation, I cannot trust her back in my salon. She proceeds to deflect any blame, sending me a ten-page text message accusing me of making her feel uncomfortable, saying I took advantage of her in a fragile state after just having a baby, telling me that I'm a terrible business owner and, in an attempt to hit below the belt, tells me that I'm not as good of a colorist as I think I am. And as all liars do, she resorts to Jesus, telling me she will pray for me and my horrible soul. Maybe it was Jesus who put that bottle in her purse because it certainly was not me.

And just when you think it's over, she showed up the next day to return the product, saying she will not support my business. And yes, she will continue to pray for me. Good! With clients like her, I'll need all the prayers I can get!

Karma mile-high club

One busy summer day, a male client of mine called to see if I could accommodate his hot new girlfriend for a haircut. Happy to see he was back out in the dating world after a recent breakup, I found time to accommodate her that day. Apparently they came from a lunch date, and both arrived a little tipsy. He was showing her around the salon, introducing her to all the staff members. He then took her into our bathroom and proceeded to spend about fifteen minutes locked in there with her.

Knowing what was probably going on, we were paralyzed. We didn't know what else to do but wait for them to come out. And eventually, they did…disheveled, laughing, and hardly even embarrassed.

Needless to say, we went through a gallon of bleach and a whole container of Lysol wipes to clean that bathroom, removing any inkling of their time in there. It was the last time I ever saw him again. I couldn't believe he would do that in my home, and I think he knew it. I couldn't look at him after that. My demeanor definitely changed, and I'm sure once he sobered up, he regretted it and knew he overstayed his welcome.

Emergency service

I'm in the middle of cutting my client's hair one evening when two firemen barged into the salon, telling us there was a possible gas leak in the building and that we needed to gather our things and evacuate as soon as possible. Although we knew they were serious, and we needed to comply with their safety demands, I saw the look of disappointment on my client's face, knowing that the haircut she was so excited to get and waited so long for would be half done. I told the fireman I couldn't leave until I was finished. I just needed another minute or two, and when I completed the haircut, we joined everyone outside.

You should've seen the puzzled look on the faces of these male firemen. They could not comprehend that I would risk my life to finish the job. Now *that's* commitment! Risking my life for my client. She was so happy. It was almost worth dying for (and for the record, it was a false alarm, so no lives were harmed).

Arrested development

A lady waltzes into the salon without an appointment, expecting an immediate consultation. She was referred by a long-standing client of mine. The desk manager explains that I am currently busy working on a client, with a full schedule for the rest of the day, and recommends that she make an appointment for a consultation. The lady is insistent that it will only take a minute and that she will wait until I have a free moment.

Right then and there I should've known I was in trouble. She proceeded to wait about ten minutes, looking impatient, but aware that I'm not going to rush my existing client in my chair. I greet my next scheduled client and send her back to get shampooed, and I call this lady over for her "quick" consultation. Mistake number 1. I hear every horror story about how no one could ever get her color right, why she left her last salon, and all about what she wants and doesn't want. This quick consultation parlayed into a ten-minute whining session.

I politely told her that I was very busy and needed to return to my scheduled client. I explained that I am not taking on any new clients at this time, and even if I would, she would have to wait three to four weeks for an appointment. She insisted that she would wait because her good friend told her to come see me. The friend in question had been a loyal client for over twenty years, and I'm not sure why I caved, but I did. That was mistake number 2.

She did wait four weeks for her appointment. Showed up late, with some cockamamie excuse about traffic, that she got off at the wrong exit—whatever. I assess her hair, which is brassy and overly oxidized from months of not getting color. It's dry and brittle like a Brillo pad, and the shape is way overgrown. She tells me that she wants a lot of blonde highlights with dimension and, of course, no brassiness.

I *clearly* explain to her that in order to eliminate brassiness, I needed to deepen her color to a soft light brown to even out her base color. *Yes*, her color might seem dark at first, but once we condition her dry locks to equalize the porosity, I would go right back in and safely highlight her hair. We would then recondition posthighlight to seal the cuticle to ensure the health of her hair. I expressed that she might not appear to be as blonde as she would like today, but within several days after she properly washed and conditioned her hair, she would notice the color naturally becoming lighter. I thoroughly explained that due to the dryness of her hair, I was guarded as to how heavily I should highlight because I was concerned that this intense color process would compromise the integrity of her hair, essentially causing her hair to break. And if after a few weeks if it did not feel light enough and *only* if her hair seemed healthy, I would have her come in and add a few more highlights to satisfy the blonder look she wanted. The journey of point A to point B can sometimes experience some traffic, but if she was on board with all of that, we could proceed. She said she fully understood and agreed, so off we went.

Standing over a client for the amount of time you have to be in order to execute a big color project, you learn a lot about them due to the conversation you have during their session. And, boy, did I learn a lot. First off, my feeling of regret was so strong, I wanted to wiggle my nose and disappear like Samantha on *Bewitched* because all she did was complain. Complained about her child who chooses not to speak to her and the friends that she refuses to spend time with. Complained about a restaurant that she had a *terrible* experience in recently and spoke about the terrible review she gave them. She tried to gossip about my client, her "good friend" who referred her, talking bad about her life and family. She admitted that the last salon she went to asked her not to come back, which she wasn't planning to anyway because—surprise, surprise—they could never get her hair to her satisfaction. Bitch, moan, repeat.

She refused to allow my assistant to use conditioner on her hair because "she hates that stuff." She didn't win that battle because I told her if we couldn't condition her hair, it would be a knotty mess, and I wouldn't be able to highlight as planned. Told me with pride all about every bad review that she has posted for other businesses because, in her words, "giving a bad review is the consumer's right to warn others that a business isn't worth going to." Just hearing that statement come out of her mouth, the hair on my neck stood up, and I knew mistake number 3 was in the process of happening. If complaining was an Olympic sport, this lady was a gold-medal winner. I say a prayer to get through the next few hours, and I finish her service.

Upon completion, she is satisfied. She expresses that she would've liked to have seen more blonde, but she agrees to be patient and trust me that it will get lighter with a few washes. Once again, I promise her that we will wait two weeks, and once I see how her overall texture has held up, I have no problem adding in a few more highlights if need be.

She pays her bill, tips both my assistant and myself, and even happily lingers a few minutes more to finish a conversation she was having with the next client in my chair. All is good in my world. She is done and relatively happy. I begin to think I might've just pulled this off, so proud of myself for possibly making this kvetchy lady happy!

Listen, she might be a royal pain in the ass, but as a professional, I am groomed to deal with all types of personalities, so I treat her with the professional courtesy I extend to everyone who sits in my chair. And I covered all my bases, spoke very honestly and directly to her at all stages of her service, and gave her advice as to the proper care for her hair at home. Also, if a client seems remotely unhappy, I would never accept a gratuity from them because I would not feel comfortable accepting one until they were. You can't refuse to work on a client just because she's a negative Nelly, if you are good and worth your salt, you can break an old dog of their annoying tricks. Or so I thought.

Fast-forward to 10:00 a.m. the next morning. I'm unlocking the door to start the day, and the phone is ringing. It's her, and she ain't happy. Sixteen hours later, and she's calling to complain. She's already left two messages on our voicemail, and per our caller ID, this is her seventh call to the salon, and it's only 10:00 a.m.

I let the desk manager deal with this. I have to get ready to start my clients for the day. Unfortunately, it was a while before I could call this lady back because I knew this would not be a quick call, so I wanted to do it when I had more time. But true to form for such a skutch, she called four more times throughout the day, inquiring why I hadn't called her back as of yet.

When we finally spoke, she badgered me for over twenty minutes, insisting that she is coming back ASAP to add more highlights. I explain that I was concerned that rehighlighting this soon would compromise the integrity of her hair, and her hair would break off. She proceeds to yell at me, "*I know* what is good for *my* hair, *not you.*"

Regardless of my retort, this is never going to end with this woman until I do as she wants, and if I don't, it will only result in her favorite pastime—a social media bashing. Upon her refusal to listen to reason, she says she will take full responsibility if anything happens to her hair. I explain that if I agree, she will be instructed to sign a waiver that relieves me of any responsibility for any further damage that not *might* but *will* occur by bleaching her hair this soon. She agrees. Mistake number 4.

She arrives the next day, attitude like a diva. I hand her the contract waiver that I drew up, covering every little detail, removing me of any responsibility from that moment forward once I touch her hair, which I am doing under duress. She is instructed to initial each bullet point and sign along with my signature and, as a witness, the signature of my manager. After reading it for over twenty minutes, she began to nitpick the waiver, arguing things we discussed on the phone that I included to protect me and my business.

That's the final straw for me. I'm not feeling comfortable with her attitude and remind her that she agreed to sign this waiver supplied by me in order to service her. I express that I feel this type of behavior is like a game for her, and as the business owner, I have the right to refuse her service, which I decided was best in this situation.

Like the Joker, she literally laughed in my face and told me that she's not leaving my salon until I redo her hair. And if that wasn't ballsy enough, she proceeds to tell me that she recorded our phone conversation from the day before, and if I don't fix her hair, she will sit on my couch all day long and tell everyone who walks in that I am a terrible business owner. I laugh at her ridiculousness, tell her to be my guest, and I retreat to the back room to enjoy a leisurely lunch, using up all that time I put aside for this woman's appointment.

She continued to sit on my couch for another hour until she realized she wasn't going to win this battle with me. That's when she upped her game and decided to call the police! When they arrived, she wanted them to force me to fix her hair or get them to make me refund her money back. The cop shook his head at this nutjob, realizing this was no crime, just an uptight Karen wanting to get her way. He said he was sorry that she wasn't happy that her hair didn't come out the way she wanted; told her that if she wasn't satisfied when she had it done days ago, she shouldn't have paid her bill; and escorted her out.

To my surprise, that was the last I ever heard of her. No bad Yelp review, no dispute for the charges for her service from her credit card company. But a huge lesson learned. Trust your gut. If it walks like a duck and quacks like a duck, it's a fucking duck.

Squirrel patrol

On a delightful spring day, we decided to open our front door to breathe a burst of fresh air. The flowers were blooming, the breeze felt great, and it felt good to sit in the salon with our doors opened on a busy day.

As I was finishing a haircut, I glanced an image on the floor by the base of my chair, and I saw some kind of small creature with a long tail. I immediately figured it was some kind of rodent, and that's all it took for me to run away to the front desk and jump up on the chair.

To our surprise, a baby squirrel entered our salon, probably displaced from its mother, and sat in the middle of the busy chaos, looking around. Our new friend was very docile and seemed very comfortable among us. My staff tried for almost an hour to coax it toward the front door by making a potato chip trail, and he was happy for the snack but not willing to leave.

In comes my next client for his appointment, who sensed our dilemma. With his quick thinking, he grabbed a small wastebasket and lid and swiftly scooped him up into it, safely depositing our little furry friend outside where he belonged and closed our door to deter other strays from entering.

We like to say we had a Karma mascot for a moment, but we hope our furry little friend found his way back to his momma.

Knots landing

A young girl came in on a Friday afternoon for a haircut. As she walks to the shampoo area to get washed for her appointment, her mother casually tells the hairdresser that the child has a small knot at the underneath part of her hair. Correction: that tangle was the size of a wasp's nest! The mom was not aware how bad the knot was because the child kept her hair tied back all the time.

To cut it off would consist of removing two thirds of the hair on her head, so unfortunately, this poor child had to endure *three hours* at the sink, with three of my employees feverishly trying to detangle this mess. She took it like a champ and patiently dealt with the excruciating discomfort of all of that combing. The stylists who took on this task somehow got it done but were absolutely exhausted, and their hands ached for days afterward.

The original Karen

A long-standing client of mine, who had been with me before I opened my own salon, was having a difficult time understanding my new role and responsibilities as I transitioned from just a hairdresser to the owner of a business. She was a tough bird and was always demanding full attention whenever she was present. She didn't seem to understand, nor did she care about the new stress I was under, where I was not only focused on the client in my chair but also on every little issue and the curveballs I was being thrown each day. She felt I wasn't giving her the attention and the courtesy she felt so deserving of, so she requested to conference me privately in my bathroom to talk.

In that tiny little bathroom, she accused me of being a terrible business owner, saying I was rude to her and that my personality changed since I opened my salon. I have dealt with this woman as she would command full attention in my salon many times, which is the same diva behavior she displayed in the previous salon we worked in, where she was asked not to come back. This lady does not know how to wait her turn and completely disregards the paying client in my chair to ask a ridiculous question about a restaurant recommendation or to ask where I bought the shoes I wore last Wednesday. She had enough of me, and I was certainly done dealing with her as well.

I let her finish her tirade, and when she was done, it was my turn. I apologized that she felt this way and calmly explained that although my attitude wasn't to her liking, owning a business was a stress she would never understand. I brought to her attention that she expects the record to screech on the jukebox when she walks into the room. I told her that she is rude as well when she doesn't get the attention she wants, and I was tired of her disregarding my business practices whenever she was in my salon.

We broke up that day and many other times throughout these past seventeen-plus years. She started to come in on days that I wasn't in, which I guess is her way of getting what she wants without having to deal with me. And when I work on the day of her appointment, she cannot contain her dismay and declares out loud, "Why is she here?"

Size matters

So I have a tendency to be very detailed in my tutorials when explaining to a client how to properly style their hair. I demonstrate on my own head, teach them useful tips to make styling easier, and use food references when I talk about the size of how much product to use—molding paste the size of a pea, styling gel like a Hershey's Kiss, pumped-out mousse the size of an egg. Most understand due to those references, yet one client took it literally.

It's a busy day, and my desk manager comes over to speak to me. She's laughing and shaking her head as she walks my way and says, "I'm so sorry to interrupt you, but there is a client on the phone, and she has a question. She was in with you the other day, and when you put mousse in her hair, you told her to use the size of an egg. She brought an egg into the bathroom to be sure she used the right amount. She uses jumbo-sized eggs. Did you mean that size?"

Does it matter? Absolutely not, but if this lady is bringing eggs into the bathroom to be sure to get it right, she earned the right to speak to me directly on the phone. I excuse myself from the client in my chair and pick up the phone. I jokingly apologized to her for not making the exact size reference at the time and, without laughing, reassured her that she was smart to call me because if she used mousse the size of a large egg, it wouldn't have worked the same!

Massage envy

I worked in a salon/spa earlier in my career. Aside from hair and nails, they offered massages as well. It was a reputable establishment, no hanky-panky going on there, until that one fateful day, a male client, who also frequented the hair salon, was in, getting a massage. The therapist completed the session and left him in the room to dress. He came to the reception desk, paid for his service, gave her a tip, and left.

She returned to the room to find a very obvious mess on the sheets. Immediately angered by the deliberate state it was left for her to clean, she told our boss what had occurred and who the client was.

Our boss was fuming at the audacity that this man had. He took such pride in the holistic nature of the massage department that he was completely offended. He called the man on the phone and told him that he knew what he did and that he was not allowed back to our salon for any services anymore.

The next day, the man called back to speak with the boss. He apologized and explained that he had an ED problem and was seeking help from a urologist to fix it. Being a man himself, my boss started to sympathize with the guy, knowing how uncomfortable that could be. But then the guy asked if he could still come get massaged if he brought his own sheets. He lost his privileges. Absolutely not!

Off-duty nurse

I'm in the middle of highlighting a client's hair, and I realize I'm not feeling so great. Out of nowhere, I begin to feel dizzy, and I break out in a sweat. Trying to remain calm and not to panic anyone around me, I excuse myself to the back room for a minute. I take off my stylist robe and remove my sweater to cool down. The room began to spin, and down I went.

My coworkers heard a loud noise and pried open the door, finding me passed out on the ground. Although no one was sure what to do, they immediately start elevating my feet and getting me juice, a cold compress, anything to try to help me in that situation.

As I'm coming to, over the concerned shoulders of my coworkers, I see my client with half her head in foils, waving her arms around like a nut, asking if I'm going to be able to finish her hair! They are looking at her in disbelief because she's not offering any help or showing any concern as to why I might've fainted. Instead, she's in full panic that only half of her head was foiled and that her hair will not be finished properly for her nephew's wedding that weekend.

I'm starting to feel a bit better, and I just can't stand to listen to her any longer, so I get up and finish foiling the remaining section of her head. I give my assistant instructions on how to finish and leave to go home with my husband, who was called by the salon manager as soon as this happened.

Hours later, at the end of that day, the crazy foil lady called the salon, and when the manager realized it was her on the phone, she immediately figured this woman must be calling to check in to see how I was doing. Nope, not at all. She was calling to ask what shampoo the assistant used on her because she loved the smell so much, she wanted to come in the next day to purchase one for herself. Crazy, right?

It gets better. As I'm home resting, I realize that the panicked, unhelpful client is an emergency room nurse, a qualified professional who would've known exactly what to do in that situation, who should've elbowed her way past all of my colleagues and began checking my pulse and following in her nursing oath! I guess that day, she was off duty, which is what I became whenever she tried to get another appointment.

Mind your business

I got married when I was rather young to a guy fifteen years older than me, which must've led many to believe I'd be having kids right away due to his older age. I didn't usually share my decision to not have children with many people simply because they might not understand my feelings. One client in particular was fascinated with asking me if I was pregnant every time she visited the salon. She was pretty opinionated about the age gap between my husband and me and was insistent that I should hurry up and get pregnant because he wasn't getting any younger. Every time I would see her, she would tell me that his sperm was probably weakening from his age and that my eggs were getting old. She was known to be pushy and insert herself in other people's business where she didn't belong, and it was hard to avoid. All I could do is just smile and laugh it off.

Around the same time that this badgering had taken place, my best friend was a few years into her fertility journey without any luck. I knew firsthand her struggles and disappointment when each procedure would not work and was there to support her along the way.

One particular day, I see the client parking her car across the street and make her way toward our door. I just heard from my girlfriend that unfortunately her third round of IVF did not work, so I was upset for her and annoyed that I'd have to deal with the intrusive questions from this yenta.

Like clockwork, she started in with the questions. Instead of rolling my eyes and yelling at her, I decided to take a different approach. I thought of how upset my friend would've felt if someone asked her such an insensitive question during this tough time and knew that this woman needed to be stopped. I motioned for her to come close so she would know that I wanted to tell her something in private. I used my friend's story as if it was me and told her that I was unable to get pregnant. I explained that I was only telling her because she constantly asked whenever she saw me, and I would appreciate it if she would please stop.

This woman's jaw hit the floor, she stuttered an apology and was so embarrassed that she couldn't even look at me, and she should be. No one should involve themselves in such a private matter. You never know the struggle someone is going through and have no right to inquire about the choices one makes for themselves. I think she learned a valuable lesson to mind her own business because she never asked me again…or anyone else for that matter.

Blow job

Getting a haircut can be an itchy experience for some, especially if you have coarse hair. And no matter how hard we try, those little wiry suckers always seem to sneak down into the cape making the client itchy and uncomfortable.

I had an 8-year-old client, whose hair was as thick and coarse as a Brillo pad. We had a routine that when I was done with the initial buzz portion halfway through his haircut, I would carefully open the cape and wipe away any cut hairs. Then I'd sprinkle good old Pinaud Clubman talc powder on his neck and down his shirt, and use the blow-dryer to blow it away.

His dad brought him in for his haircut one busy Saturday afternoon, and as I was cutting the boy's hair, the dad and I were engrossed in a conversation. The boy is squirming around and whining about being itchy, asking me to blow the powder down his back. I'm still cutting and paying attention to the haircut, but admittedly focused on my discussion with his dad so it was falling on deaf ears. Well, this little boy felt he was ignored long enough. Out of nowhere, he yelled out "Nik, are you gonna blow me or what??" With that, the whole salon got quiet, the dad's eyes popped right out of his head, astonished at what his child requested. He did not know what our hair cutting routine was, nor did anyone else in the room, leaving them all to think the same dirty thing!

Grandpa Fabio

A few years back, when I was having some health issues, I had to cut back on my work schedule. I had a seizure one morning while at work, resulting in a four-day hospital stay. The doctors were still unaware as to why I was having these transient-ischemic-attack episodes, and they sometimes came on so fast, I never knew when to expect them. All of my clients had to be accommodated by my other stylists at the last minute and were grateful to be taken care of but were more concerned for my health than their hair upon hearing the news—all but one client.

He seemed mildly concerned but was perturbed that his appointment had to be canceled and refused to be accommodated by anyone else but me. He insisted that he be told the moment I come back to work so he could come in to see me. Apparently, he had a vacation coming up, and he needed to be seen before he left on his holiday, which took top billing over my hospital stay. They offered him an appointment with anyone else on my staff, and Fabio kept refusing, saying he only trusted my work.

I came back to work for a few hours the following week, and only because he badgered my desk every day to see when I'd be in, I decided to give him an appointment just to accommodate him once and for all. You would think he was a male model, doing a front-page photo shoot on location in the Maldives, right? Nope, just a male version of a Karen, a regular middle-aged guy with a huge ego that apparently makes a career out of being difficult.

Well, He must've had a lunch date with the president that day because the time I offered wasn't good for him. Back on the wait list he went. He proceeded to call the salon the next morning and told my desk manager that he went somewhere else for his haircut and had the audacity to say, "Tell Nikki when she gets her shit together to call me, and I'll come back."

Needless to say, I'd be using my scissors in a different way if he ever tried to sit in my chair ever again.

35,000-foot rescue

I decided to go away for the extended Fourth of July weekend, and against my better judgment, I took off from work on a Saturday. It was a busy day at the salon, and for the first time, I was leaving everyone behind to work without me. It was 9:15 a.m., and already, the temperature was nearly ninety degrees, so it was going to be a hot one that day. I'm boarding a flight to Key West, and my phone rings. It's my salon manager. "I hate to bother you, but the air-conditioning isn't working. It's eighty-eight degrees in the salon."

I could hardly hear her on the phone. Apparently, the salon was in an uproar. The clients were standing on chairs trying to reach the air-conditioning unit in an attempt to fix it, to no avail. The plane was just about ready to take off. The flight attendant is starting her dissertation on how to use your seat as a flotation device in case of an emergency and is staring at me to turn my phone off. I can't leave them in the lurch like this. I'm in full panic, knowing how busy they are and how horrible it must be for everybody there to work in such uncomfortable conditions, *especially* with me away on vacation.

As the plane was taking off, my husband snuck in a call to his friend who is an HVAC repairman, who usually works in NYC every day. By the grace of God, he had a job that morning in Long Island, and as a favor to my husband, he left that job and rushed over to my salon, and within an hour, it was fixed.

A text came through midflight from my manager of a thumbs-up and a snowflake emoji, so I knew I made it happen. So even at thirty-five thousand feet in the air, I'm still putting out fires and making sure things run smoothly at the salon. When I knew the crisis was averted, I flagged down the flight attendant with the drink cart and got a double vodka to calm my nerves and resumed back to vacation mode.

Detention

It is not uncommon for a stylist to run a few minutes late. Although we aim not to, it usually is out of our control. Sometimes certain work takes longer than expected, or maybe we were short staffed that day and it backed me up. Regardless of the reason, it unfortunately happens from time to time. But like JetBlue, I can begin a service a little late but catch up and still manage to get you out in time.

I'm finishing up a complex color service, and I ran about 15 minutes late for my next client. I apologized for my delay upon greeting her and went right to work getting her color application started. I got her out right on schedule, and she left happy and never said a word about the late start.

Fast forward 5 weeks later, she's back in my schedule for her root touch up at 12pm. It's 12:05pm and she's not here. 12:10pm, I begin to worry that she might've forgotten she had an appointment. 12:12pm, she walks in the door and as I greet her, I express my concern and mention that she was a few minutes late for her appointment. She looked me with this odd smirk and obnoxiously said "Well, you were 12 minutes late for me last time, so…you know…". This lady sat in her car and purposely waited exactly 12 minutes to come in, as her cruel way of getting even with me for my tardiness a few weeks before. Although I wanted to punish her right back by taking it out on her hair, as the true professional that I am, I didn't. But I did explain to her how foolish it was to purposely piss off the person who was now in charge of mixing chemicals to put on her head.

Good head

Hairdresser lingo can easily be misinterpreted as sexual conversation. We've had many clients look embarrassed by some of the stylist vocabulary we use in the salon. I'll ask one of my employees, "Are you going to blow her now, or can I do her first?" or tell my assistant, "Wet her down and massage it in."

The look of embarrassment on the clients' faces are priceless because although we mean it in stylist terms, it sounds erotic and naughty, like Mr. Furley overhearing a conversation at the Regal Beagle from an episode of *Three's Company*.

My assistant was washing one of my male clients. She was young and very naive about sex and all the discussion about it. She was known for her relaxing shampoo skills, and the treatment she gave this client was no exception. He sat up after his washing and joked that the shampoo was so enjoyable that he might need a cigarette. He was a longtime customer with a funny, twisted sense of humor. I knew he would appreciate the sarcasm, so I joked that my assistant was known for giving good head, by which I meant washing hair, but you can understand the undertone of the joke.

Hours later, she is washing another male client, a quiet, conservative man who hardly even spoke even while he was receiving a haircut. Apparently, he must've had a stressful day at work, and her shampooing skills were helping to relax his nerves. He sat up when it was over, thanked her, and politely complimented her skills. All of a sudden, she blurted out, "I know, I give good head."

The whole salon got quiet, and that man turned red with embarrassment. I took her aside and told her she shouldn't just say that, but she didn't understand why. I told her what it really meant with the hair joke aside, and she cringed in horror at the thought of it.

An offer I couldn't refuse

We offer plenty of options to our clients when they are either waiting for their appointment or as their chemical service is processing. We supply coffee, tea, or water and always have magazines, candies, or cookies around to satisfy their needs while they wait. So when we ask a client if there is anything we can get them while they wait, it's good to assume they would understand what we have to offer—or maybe not…

One busy day, I finished applying a clients root touch-up. My next client has arrived and just began getting shampooed for her haircut. I'm carefully cleaning off the remnants of color from the client's forehead as she's reading a magazine, and I say, "I'll be doing a haircut in my other chair while you process. Is there anything I can get you?"

"Yes," she answers. She turns and reaches into her pocketbook, pulls out a $20, and says, "I'd love a slice of pizza from the place up the block. Oh and a Diet Coke from the fountain, no ice." And she returned to her *People* magazine. I'm left standing there with her $20 in my hand, trying to figure out if she actually wants *me* to go get it for her. She must be serious because she is so consumed with her magazine that she doesn't even look up. I've always thought if someone is ballsy enough to ask such a ridiculous request. It's my job to fulfill it. I look toward the client getting shampooed in the sink and see that she's got a few minutes to go, so still in shock, I put on my jacket and walk to the pizzeria. Even the pizza guy couldn't believe I satisfied this woman's request. When I returned, she accepted her lunch with a smile, like it was part of my job description. I mean, I did say *anything,* so I guess she figured it couldn't hurt to ask.

Salon Ownership: The Grass Is Always Greener

I ventured into salon ownership simply because I was so miserable working for the salon owners I had in the past. It was an uphill battle. I was becoming increasingly unhappy at work, and I just wasn't willing to fight it anymore. The conditions at the salon were so toxic, and I felt like I was stuck aboard a sinking ship.

My husband and I had just built a house, and I really didn't have the funds to finance a venture like this, but I guess misery is a great motivator. I scraped up the funds, sacrificed a lot, and figured out a way to do it. All I wanted was a small place that I could take care of my clients in a peaceful yet professional setting. My clients were becoming miserable at the salon where I worked, and I knew if I didn't make a move soon, I would lose them.

Thankfully, my husband, Joey, is very handy and was able to transform a nearby small office space into a boutique salon. I figured out what products to stock, got it functional and ready, and started up almost immediately after quitting my other job. No rest for the weary.

Taking on the responsibility of a salon meant that I would still have to work equally as hard behind the chair and add numerous hours a week to run the joint. I couldn't cut back my volume of clients because we needed every dime I brought in to pay our overhead and my occurred start-up debt, along with paying salaries, supplies, accountants, advertising, etc.

My entire clientele followed me, so my start-up was better than others would experience if they were just starting a salon from scratch. The clients were so elated to come to our salon, happy to transition to a better environment.

Sounds easy, but trust me, it wasn't. My usual eight- to ten-hour day for five days a week turned into fifteen-hour days at least six days a week. There's no handbook to new salon ownership. This was a learning curve I had to painfully endure. A daily ritual of working out the kinks, usually while I had clients in my chair. Endless nights trying to figure out the bookkeeping aspect of the business. Days spent fixing things that may get broken, dealing with scheduling issues, and doing everything I could think of to get it on its feet. And a bill waiting to be paid for all of it. But it was mine, and I was proud of it. It was worth the effort and the lack of sleep. And as a bonus, I lost ten pounds because in all of that chaos, I never had time to eat.

It was a tricky transition going from coworker to boss for some of my staff. They knew me as a coworker and now had to digest the fact that I was their boss. Some were annoyed when I had to make decisions they didn't agree with or reprimand them for being late or not abiding by salon protocols. I had so many new responsibilities, and I needed them to understand what I expected of them to help me out. It was hard for me too. It's no fun feeling like the school principal and distancing myself from the social circle to focus on running a smooth operation.

I hated how I was treated working for other bosses. I dreamed of what it would be like to work for somebody who really respected their employees, someone who would always put them first. And that is what I did. I treated my employees the way I wished I had been treated and paid forward whatever good treatment I experienced as well. Making them and their careers a high priority would show them that they have a home with me, and like the mother of the group, they were safe and protected. I paid for 100 percent of any education for my staff that came our way and always kept my eyes open for new products or services we could learn and grow with. I recognized them on birthdays, spoiled them for the holidays, and orchestrated parties and dinners outside the salon to show my appreciation.

Like a momma bear, I swore that my team would never have to struggle by not having adequate supplies or dysfunction in the workplace so they would never have a reason to leave me. All the rainbows and unicorns one could ever dream of. And, man, was I stupid.

I am not going to say it didn't work for some. A select few are still with me all of these years and appreciate all that I do, but I've gotten my heart broken more times than I can count on two hands. Some didn't care at all. Some appreciated but took advantage, and the more I gave, the more they wanted. Some thought it would be exactly the same elsewhere and left. And some, I realized, couldn't be happy regardless what I did.

Many weeks, I would go without getting paid because it was more important to keep the money in the business to keep it running. I'd put orders on my own personal credit cards because I didn't have room on my business cards. It's still a struggle sometimes, but I do what I can to keep it going. I listened to the smart people I trusted around me and got a great accountant/bookkeeper to handle all the business jargon that I don't know about. I have a cleaning crew once a week to scrub down the salon to a pristine state. My team does a great job maintaining it throughout the week, but it needs a good cleaning after a few hairy days. I keep the salon fully stocked with an overabundance of supplies and even have a secondary supply of duplicate inventory at my home, so we never go empty-handed.

My business is a commission-based salon. The misconception of most is that the owner walks away with half of what the stylist brings in. Some stylists in our industry walk around feeling slighted because they believe that they do all the work, and the owner just fills their own pockets, and they couldn't be more wrong. The stylist makes their share, and the boss uses the other portion to pay the following:

- Rent
- Hair products used for each client and to stock the salon
- All color and chemical products used for services
- Salaries for the shampoo assistant and the desk manager
- Electric
- Phone/Internet
- Liability/disability insurance

- Accounting fees
- Advertising
- Coffee bar
- Janitorial/miscellaneous supplies needed to function properly
- Weekly cleaning staff
- Taxes
- Etc.

So in reality, when it's all said and done, the stylist makes 50 percent free and clear, and the owner makes approximately 15 to 20 percent if they are lucky.

I wish on every penny I find in the street that I could go back to being a stylist who just works behind the chair and gets their commission without doing any of the background work. It was so much easier back then when I worked for someone else and only worried about the client in my chair. Walk into the salon in the morning, pick up my scissors, and start; put them down at night, gather your shit, and leave. Only if they ventured into it themselves would they ever understand. I always believed the only way someone will appreciate all that you do is when you are not there doing it anymore. I've had the satisfaction of some of my former employees who left us for greener pastures come back later on to tell me that it wasn't. My husband has always said that I might not be the best boss, but there is nobody better. And sad for most, they have to learn that for themselves.

Being an owner means that you eat, sleep, breathe your business. Wash, rinse, and repeat. It's like a child who will never grow up and will require the same amount of effort today as it did on the first day you opened. And like the parent, when the crisis arises, the kid looks for you to fix it.

It's your responsibility to always put your business first. Keep your eyes open for opportunities for your employees to grow. Think of ways to increase revenue and stimulate client growth. Make sure everything is perfectly intact before you dare to take any time off. Regardless if you are away on vacation, they are to be paid on time in full as usual. This business *is* your child. The only way it will function is because you do it.

Looking back now, I'll admit I thought it was going to be easy. So young and stupid I was. I figured if the current boss I had could do it, of course I could too. She didn't care the way I would and was absent most of the time, so I thought I had this in the bag. And I know that I've done a good job, but, boy, this was far from easy.

Anyone venturing into something like this should know that anything worthwhile isn't easy. Whether it be a small beauty studio or suite or a big-time, full-capacity salon, your life will be consumed from that moment on, and you will probably make less money than you did when you were just an operator behind the chair. You'll spend your mornings before work running from store to store to get toilet paper or twenty-volume developer or any miscellaneous item you are in need of. Make last-minute scheduling changes when someone is sick or decides to quit. Unclog the toilet while your client is having their color washed off. You will lie awake in bed strategizing all the dilemmas you will face that next day, knowing you will become Winston Wolf to fix it all. Jumping into immediate work mode at the early morning ping of a text message from a client who needs to cancel or from one of your employees who can't make it in that day. It all comes back to you.

I'm still not certain if I would do it all over again, go into starting up a new salon, knowing what I know now, especially in these new times. The industry has changed so much in thirty-five years, and the mindset of current stylists has altered into thinking that going out on their own is the way to go. The new generation of budding stylists do not want to hustle the way we did in our earlier years, and they look at that concept as unnecessary. The loyalty to be part of a team is not what it once was, which is an emotional risk.

I'll admit it has been an exhausting yet very rewarding journey for me. The good will always cancel out the bad, but it's lonely at the top. The struggles I go through come with the territory of owning any kind of service business. It's all for the customers, and the sacrifice was all mine. Was it worth it in the end? I guess time will tell. And just as I begin to doubt my future as a boss, ready to throw in the towel and find a job working for someone else, I hug another happy client goodbye at the end of their service. And as they warmly thank me for supplying them with a great experience in our professional environment, I begin to forget the pain.

Blindsided

And just when you think you have it all figured out, the rug gets pulled out right from under you. As a boss, you do everything you need to do to keep the work environment functional. You supply your staff with everything they need to make their work life easier. You educate your team with anything you can find to help keep them at the top of their game. You compensate them whenever you can and gift them for birthdays and holidays to show your appreciation for the hard work that they do. Orchestrate dinners and gatherings outside of the workplace to keep the personal level intact to help balance the professional aspect of long hours working closely together. You sacrifice your own needs by putting them before yourself to be sure they are happy in the workplace. It's a hard pill to swallow when you know you covered your end of the bargain, and they pack up their things and leave you anyway.

I thought I was approachable and observant enough to know the signs, but with all the responsibilities you have as a boss, it's easy to lose perspective when you're focusing on trying to get the job done. Before I could see what was happening, it was too late. No reason, no notice, just me left behind in an empty salon, sitting in a pool of my own tears. I'm like the Taylor Swift of salon bosses. I take them along on a great journey, and unfortunately, they break my heart. They'll leave for no reason whatsoever. But then I write a song about them and get my own satisfaction.

This heartbreak happened recently. I mentored her since she was a kid. She was an assistant working with me at another salon, and I took her under my wing because our boss was taking advantage of her. I paid for all of her continued education and brought her with me as my next in line when I opened my salon. She was a hardworking young single mom with a great work ethic. I trusted her opinion at all times and valued her as my moral compass in many salon situations.

We had the most amazing work relationship for over twenty years, or so I thought, until she asked to speak with me at the end of a busy workday. She told me she was unhappy and was leaving effective immediately to go out on her own. My ears went deaf. I couldn't quite comprehend what she was saying, or maybe I didn't want to believe this was really happening. Her reasons did not make sense. She claimed she felt second-best to other employees, which couldn't have been further from the truth. She said she wanted to grow in a different way, to be out on her own. None of it made any sense. She had already committed to her new path and signed it away on the dotted line.

When I look back now, it still feels like a bad dream. She was leaving me after all of these years to open up her own salon suite and taking a bunch of my clients with her. No notice, no heart-to-heart conversation to let me in on her feelings, and no opportunity for me to try to make her happy enough to stay. She had it all set up already by the time she quit. And to make matters worse, it was around the block from my salon. Over twenty years of working alongside somebody, and you are left feeling like you never really knew them.

How much does she hate me that she would want to leave and even worse, go behind my back and set up shop a stone's throw away to hurt me and my business like this? Where did I go wrong? What could I have done to keep her? Why couldn't she sit me down and talk to me if she was not happy? Where was her head at when she decided this was the best decision for her, knowing that she was flushing a twenty-plus-year relationship down the drain? I guess I will never know.

If she had given me some notice, told me that this was her dream, and was going to leave regardless, of course I would've been heartbroken. But the way she had it all set up for weeks behind my back, she literally broke my heart. What is a boss to do in a situation like this? I had to wipe away the tears, put on my big-girl bloomers, and get back behind that chair and make it work.

This is why as a salon owner, I feel it's very important to never leave the chair. Some salon owners sift their clientele into the stylist chairs and take on managerial roles instead of actually servicing clients. In a moment like this, if you are no longer servicing clients and the hairdresser decides to leave you, you will watch every single client walk out your door. I think it's important for a salon owner who, at one time, was an active hairdresser to maintain the physical work behind the chair because when the chips are down, you have to be able to swoop in and accommodate everyone to keep them.

As a salon owner, I do not own the path of any of my employees. They all have the right to leave to make themselves happy if they feel they need to. The way my business was molded, I never thought I would've needed noncompete contracts to protect me from employees walking out and setting up shop a block away. We were family, and I trusted it all on a handshake that this couldn't happen to me.

I do have a rule in my salon. If you are not happy here, then you can't stay. But that is why I have gone above and beyond to try to make them happy on all levels so they shouldn't want to leave. Maybe the grass *is* greener. Maybe I expect too much from them. Maybe I can't give them what they actually need. Or maybe I make it look so easy that they think they can do it themselves. Whatever the reason, I've learned it can happen even when you think it can't.

I don't think I'm ever going to get over that particular breakup. At the end of the day, it's not that she left, it's how she did it that hurt the most. I invested so much of myself into someone who I thought was on the same page as me. It feels like my husband cheated on me or as if my sister packed up her things and drove away, and I'll never see her again. Someone I trusted with the thing most dear to me, my business, disregarded my kindness and stomped on my heart. She built a career on my back, on my dime, and left feeling like she deserved it. She orchestrated an escape plan and told me at the eleventh hour after her car was packed up with all of her things, when it was too late to fix.

I was such a fool. I felt like a loser. I felt like everything I worked for and valued about my myself as a salon owner was a sham. What the hell did I know about running a successful business if a person I put the most faith in left me for no reason whatsoever. Who was going to be next? And reflecting back to the experiences I had with my former bosses and recognizing that although I left them for my own reasons, they gave far less and had employees remain loyal and stay with them for years. I thought if I did it differently and worked hard to keep my staff happy and keep the salon running to perfection, no one would dream of leaving. I gave them everything I never had. And where did it get me?

Sure, I had plenty of people quit my business over the years, and some I had to fire. It had many wondering if I was as bad as Miranda Priestly from *The Devil Wears Prada*, but the truth is, running a salon is a tough undertaking. I'm a stickler for rules and have high expectations for my staff, but my positives greatly outweigh my negatives. I treat my workers with respect, buy them breakfast every week, pay them more than other salons pay, compensate extra when extra work is done, extravagant gifts for holidays, paid vacation, and provide them with a safe work environment. And if they desired a back rub to stay, then get me the massage oil, I'll do it. All I ask in return is to be loyal and honest, do the job with a strong work ethic, and take good care of my clients. Sounds easy, right?

This was the most humbling thing I could've ever gone through. I'm not a superhero boss, just a hardworking girl who owns a business that she loves, who clearly doesn't have it all figured out. Salons are like the ocean. You turn your back on it, and it'll knock you down. Even if you're paying attention, it can be pulled right out from under you, just like this situation. I thought I had it all worked out, and then I watched it all walk out the door.

I guess the best lesson will be how I get through it. Life is full of curveballs. It's out of your control, and there's no way to avoid it. And although my life had been turned upside down, I need to stay on track and focus on my original mission. Get behind that chair, pick up those magical scissors, and continue to make the clients beautiful.

What I Have Learned

So at the end of the day, I am merely still just a person, still tired, still full of hair, still dehydrated and stained with hair color, just older. Because as exhausted as I might be, I will drive home thinking about what excitement the next day will have in store for me. And yes, there will probably be a bag of fast food to accompany me home. As tiring as it can be, I couldn't think of anything else I would rather do. Nothing else I could ever dream of to muster this type of strength to accomplish. I think I was born to do this. Or the verdict is in—I am clinically insane.

After all the years piled up as an assistant, a stylist, and an owner, I feel each day has been a lesson, a lesson on what turned out right and a master's degree as to why things didn't go as planned. You see, the biggest lesson in all of this is that you can't expect it all to turn out like it would in a book or a movie. There are so many moving parts to success. My interpretation of beauty might not be the same as the client who is paying for it. I might not have the right help or adequate time needed to properly execute a job. The client might not have explained it clearly, and I might not have dug deep enough to understand their vision.

So much could go wrong before it can be right. The lesson is to breathe deeply, slow it down, really listen, and communicate every step of their journey. And if you cannot achieve it or passionately feel it's a bad idea, be honest and say you can't. Trust your gut. If it doesn't feel right, it's not. I've had clients thank me for my honesty. No one benefits from a bad hair job. The client feels ugly, and the hairstylist loses endless nights of sleep, overthinking everything they could've done differently. Keep in mind that your reputation is at stake. One bad experience, one bad Yelp review, you're working the counter at Sally Beauty Supply, banished to a life in hair purgatory.

Working behind the chair is like performing on stage all day. Some people love to come in and be entertained by me and my Jewish schtick. Some are annoyed by me and just wish I'd just shut the fuck up so they can read their book. When clients pass over the threshold into our salon, they are leaving behind all the things they want to forget about during their visit. Some come after work from a job that they hate. Some just dropped off kids and are anxiously awaiting to revel in their free time away from their parental duties. Most know a lot about our personal lives and come in for the latest updates about our families, vacations, milestones, etc. Some are involved in bad relationships or are dealing with so much at home that they need to disappear and be entertained for a bit.

Let's face it. We all wish we were five pounds thinner and five times richer. We all have some sort of problems at home. Everyone hates their jobs, kids, spouses, or life for moments at a time, and they come to us to escape it all even if it's just for a thirty-minute haircut.

For some, their lives are lonely, and they think of us as a friend or even more like family. A reliable ear to listen or someone to give advice, a restaurant recommendation, and good hair. Or maybe they want us to be quiet and focus on the job they are expecting. We need to perform for each client, tailored to what their expectations are. We are their people. They choose us, and it feels good to be there for them.

And as much as you try your best to make your clients or your staff happy, there is no guarantee that they will stay. It's a tough pill to swallow when you think you've covered all of your bases, and they leave you anyway. That decision might not have anything to do with you, and you might be left with no explanation why. The best advice is to focus on who stays and stay true to your work. Wish them farewell, don't burn your bridges, and continue on your path.

Our career is grueling, not only physically but mentally as well. We are always *on*, always expected to be in a good mood and able to whip up a miracle in a small amount of time. Our clients look to us to make it happen, and somehow, we do, but it'll only happen if we balance it all with our own personal self-care. We need to take care of ourselves; otherwise, we are just machines, practicing the art of "wake up, work, sleep, repeat."

Find time to work out. It'll keep your body fit enough to withstand the physicality of our job. I found Pilates halfway through my career, and it was a lifesaver to keep my core strong to stand all day and to build proper muscle strength to keep my arms erect and in motion all day long. What we do requires every part of our body, and we need to listen to it and take the time to condition our bodies to maintain longevity in our field.

Get massages regularly. Our bodies cramp up, and we need to ease the tense muscles that build up in order to stay limber so we can continue. Foot massage is key. I go every week (sometimes twice) to the foot spa. Nothing feels better than sixty minutes in a dim, quiet room while someone rubs your feet, easing the pain of standing all day. Granted, I'm the idiot who insists on wearing heels all day, but even wearing sneakers or comfortable shoes, it catches up with you.

Go out and enjoy experiences in your time off. When you are back at work and getting stressed, it'll help you get through it by remembering the fun time you had a few days ago.

Try to clear your mind for a few minutes a day. Our brains are constantly put to the test, thinking, plotting, strategizing, keeping good time to stay on schedule, creating. Trust me, it'll catch up with you and take you over. It'll age you if you don't. You'll be so overwhelmed, you will start to feel like early-onset dementia is setting in. Our minds are like cars; eventually, you have to put it in park and turn the engine off. Give your head time to cool down and rest. I'm speaking from experience.

Get enough sleep. Just like our overworked brains, our bodies need to shut down and get adequate sleep. Nothing feels better than getting the proper eight hours of rest (sometimes even six will do it). It's like you recharged your batteries. Treat your body like one of your smart devices. At the end of the day, if your iPhone is at a 21 percent battery, you plug it in to charge. When it's back to 100 percent, it's good for the day. Give your entire body time to rest, so it can build back the strength to do it all over again the next day.

Do not do your friends' and family's hair at home. You need to keep the scissors where they belong. And have them come to your workspace and get it done there. You need to separate your work from your life outside of work, and it'll give them a sense of what you do all day and the responsibilities you have while you are not at home. It sounds so easy to just bring your tools home and give your sister a haircut, but you know it's *never* just one head. The next thing you know, more people are coming into the kitchen with towels on their head, lining up for "a quick trim while you're already here." Even my own husband gets his haircut at the salon, partly because he doesn't like the mess at home but mostly because he understands that I need to physically separate myself from work once I leave. Owning this business means I have so many other work responsibilities I have to focus on when I get home, and so picking up my scissors after a full day of work is borderline abusive. I learned early to separate and firmly say no. Do you ask your relatives to clean your teeth or repair your house or file your taxes after they worked all day? You are just as important as any other career, and it should be respected for the time you put into it as well. Family members must also understand that due to the fact that they usually don't pay or are getting huge breaks in fees, they cannot take up prime appointment slots. They might have to be patient and wait a bit and cannot take up a coveted Saturday morning appointment or a prime evening spot we need to reserve for our clients. But we will get them done, just *not* at home.

This is a PSA: you do not know everything you need to know. Keep learning. Get inspired by anything you see, whether it be on social media or hair industry publications. Grab on to any education you can get your hands on. Styles change every day; new products are always on the horizon. Hair color palettes are like seasons—lighter and brighter for the summer, dark and rich for the winter. Be ahead of it. You are the trusted style guru for your clients. They turn to you to know what's the trend. You stop learning, you start dying. Stay cued in on all new concepts for your clients. Stay fresh and always ready to bring something to the table for them or, in our case, the chair. I've successfully maintained the same clients for over thirty years, and the best compliment they give is I've never gotten stale. I always introduce them to new ideas to stay current and new products or trends to make their lives easier.

Find the balance of accommodating and saying no. Keep a tight noose on your schedule and don't budge to occasionally stay late to accommodate some loyal clients? They will eventually leave you and find someone who will. Be a little flexible when you can and learn who will appreciate it and who will take advantage of you. Our scissors don't just stop working at a certain time of the day. If you have to stay later or come in earlier, do it. Understand the situation and be available to accommodate. Most clients will be grateful for the extension of your schedule. However, if a client expects special accommodations on a regular basis, you have the right to say no. You are nobody's doormat. If they can't understand your boundaries, then they've lost their privileges.

Stand behind your work and take pride in your relationship with your clients. Don't just hear what they are saying. Really listen to what they want. If it's a bad idea, then communicate that respectfully. But if it is truly what they want, give it to them. If they are hell-bent on a certain style and you've expressed your opinion and have given them a dissertation on why you think it's not a good idea, you cannot be blamed in the end if, in fact, they are not happy. Sometimes clients need to actually see the error of their choice to understand, or maybe it's actually something they love. Either way, it is not our job to take liberties with their heads and do what *we* feel is best. We sometimes to have to accomplish looks we aren't very happy with in order to make them happy. At the end of the day, if they are happy, I'm happy.

We make people happy, and build their self-confidence. Nothing puts wind in your sails like looking at yourself in the mirror and liking what you see. Hairdressing is a feel-good industry. The odds are always in our favor. The client will leave looking and feeling better than they did when they walked in. If you look good, it's like a getting a B12 shot. So much of your stress and anxiety melts away; you have the energy and the confidence to conquer the world. And we did that.

As a salon owner, it is your responsibility to guide and mentor your stylists. Take them aside and pep talk them when they are falling behind or need a hand. Provide inspiration and guidance to help propel them to their next level. You are the Captain of their ship, and they look to you for support.

Add value to each client's service. Make their experience so exceptional that they wouldn't dream of sitting in another stylists chair. Go the extra mile to educate your clients about product knowledge and styling skills so they can easily duplicate your work at home. If you teach them something about their hair that they didn't know, or bring to light something they already do, it will prove that you are invested in their hair and paying attention. And that reassures a client that they made the right decision by choosing you.

If the client is not happy, don't let them leave until they are. Many times, a client has sat in my chair, and I can see the body language or the look on their face in the mirror. Regardless of your busy schedule, whether you're booked solid without any extra time, or it's the last appointment of the night and you have to leave, you do not let them leave. Do not tell them to come back another time if they are truly not satisfied because the likelihood of that is slim; they probably won't. They just paid a decent amount for a job that was subpar, and it'll feel like you shrugged them off. Once you release them to go home and inspect in their own mirror, you've lost them. They will see three other people who will reassure them that they have the right to be unhappy, which validates that you shouldn't have let them leave in the first place. And by then, they will feel indifferent to your shrug off and go elsewhere to have it corrected. Take the extra time to correct a problem, and most of the time, it's a quick fix, but it will speak volumes that you cared enough to do it.

You might not be able to make everybody happy, but you better damn well try. We are not only dealing with the dynamics of a haircut or the science behind hair color, we are dealing with living beings who chose us to take care of their beauty needs—people who have a vision and feelings, people who might be dealing with a laundry list of personal issues and are throwing it our way to make them happy.

We can't just run and fire them as clients at their first complaint. We need to take responsibility that they are genuinely not 100 percent pleased. Just because they don't like the work you do doesn't make them difficult or crazy. It's our job to have them leave with a good feeling. Even if they leave knowing their final goal might not have been met, they leave knowing we are both on that journey to get them there eventually.

Make sure the batteries in your shit detector are at full charge. If someone gives you a bad feeling, and you can sense that working on them is going to result in a problem, trust your gut and say no. You have the right to refuse service to someone who is giving off that difficult feeling. There is a small (I'm being kind, LOL) percentage of the population that is chronically never happy in any service entity and will think nothing of complaining or writing a bad review if they are dissatisfied. They are probably consistently unhappy in restaurants, stores, or anywhere that provide a service, so you are sure to be the next in line for harassment. If you see their name in your schedule, and it gives you an ill feeling in your stomach, trust your shit detector and proceed with caution. Stay professional, communicate well, and do the job that is asked. At the first sign of trouble, be direct and express to them that this is how you run your business practice, and if they are not satisfied, they should go where they can be. And when they leave, lock the door!

The boss has to be there—period, end of story. There are so many minor details that add up to the success or failure of a business. As annoying as it can be to micromanage, it is crucial to the function of a salon. And as the captain of the ship, it is the boss' job to oversee everything so it runs smoothly and efficiently. The absence of an owner/boss leads to animosity from the staff and lacks reassurance from the clients. No one likes to be on an airplane and see the captain leave the cockpit to use the bathroom. I always think, *Who's up there flying the plane?* Sure, there's always a copilot, like our salon manager or upper staff, but there's a sense of authority when the boss is there and things run effectively. Plus, it's my venture, and I will not apologize for how I need to run my business. When the boss is present, everyone does what is expected of them. When the boss is absent, things scale down a bit, and the staff goes on cruise control. Things get messy without a sense of urgency to clean, and some employees skate by doing the minimum. Like the saying goes, "when the cat's away, the mice will play."

I am extremely fortunate that I have employees who pick up my slack if I'm out and handle what needs to be handled as if I'm there. But let's be honest, when mom's car pulls off the driveway, the kids turn the volume up, put their feet up on the coffee table, and drink milk right out of the carton.

I worked for a woman who owned the salon yet didn't want to be there at all. The salon became sloppy and was poorly run due to her lack of desire to be present and lead. Air-conditioning remained broken in the summer, heat hardly working in the winter, chronic plumbing issues, checks never left for COD payment when deliveries of supplies would arrive, broken furniture—you name it. Stupid, really, because animosity builds, employees grow resentful, and it becomes anarchy. The clients felt it too. Things she would've seen if she was present or showed any interest in doing what a boss needs to do, which is why she's no longer in business. I left to open my salon, and every client I had happily left that place and followed us to our new home.

The boss wears many hats. From standing behind the chair all day cutting hair to fixing the clog in the shampoo sink. Expediting the flow of all the staff's clients receiving services throughout the day to going home to do hours of payroll and unpacking inventory orders. Creating custom hair-color masterpieces head after head to becoming the shampoo girl when we are short staffed. Let's not forget playing part-time concierge, giving out restaurant recommendations and travel advice to clients while on my hands and knees, removing color stains off the salon floor. And last but not least, becoming the salon mom-therapist, diffusing issues with coworkers and being a sounding board for clients.

Starting my own business had expanded my knowledge in so many areas, and although exhausting, it's the role I was meant to play. You have to know that before getting into it and know that sacrifices are going to be made, and your time will be limited. It's not for the weak but for the strong. It's extremely rewarding. It would be easier if I were selfish and just worried about myself, but I'm not built like that. That's too lonely of a life anyway. I need a team. I love my tribe. I was born to lead, so I put on the hat and march on.

Don't ever stop working behind the chair. As I just recently learned, if you walk away from your clients and rely on your stylists to service them, they will follow them out the door if the stylist leaves.

Lead by example and stay true to yourself. Dress the part, act the part, and don't accept anything less than you would do. It is your responsibility to mold your business into what your vision is. To others, it is just a job; to me, it's my life. It was my last dollar and my last cell of energy that went into this venture, and no one should work to deviate my path. If they try, pull the car over and let them out. You will survive without them and possibly replace them with people who are there to support your dream and be happy to do so.

So the saga continues, thirty-five years of making people beautiful. Many more to go. I'm just a hairdresser, I guess. I've spent most of my life making people happy. Why would I want to do anything else?

I'm the same as I always was, just a little older and wiser, a few more gray hairs, and a few more wrinkles, but, hey, that's what Botox is for. I take turmeric now every day for joint health. I wear glasses at work to function. Occasionally, I wear sensible shoes. I'm like a salmon swimming upstream, fighting this aging process every step of the way.

But one thing is for certain, I am never leaving this industry. I've got hair spray running through my veins. As I start my day behind the first client in my chair—in heels, of course—I silently hear Elton John sing, "I'm still standing," I'm now a veteran in my field. I've owned my salon for eighteen years and counting. I've been at this for almost thirty-five years. And after everything I've endured as a hairdresser and as an owner, I realize that I know nothing at all about this industry. You can't predict the next day or the heartaches or joys that will come.

I begin each day hopefully optimistic that all of my efforts will pay off, but I quietly hold my breath for the next dilemma that will keep me up all night. I am proud of what I have accomplished and am in awe of the changes I've seen occur over these years behind the chair. I'm grateful that my body has held up all of these years and has allowed me to continue on my journey. I'm grateful for the lessons I've learned and for the loyalty of my amazing clients throughout the years. And I'm grateful that the fast-food drive-thrus are open late.

About The Author

Nikki Silbert Cestaro started working in a hair salon at the age of fifteen years old solely because she didn't play a sport after school and needed something to keep her busy. Quickly realizing her path in the beauty business had begun, she worked her way from shampoo assistant to head salon stylist to salon owner in her thirty-five years in the industry. She has gained success at all levels and, having experienced the ups and downs of salon life, decided it was time to use her childhood love of writing to give others insight into a life behind the chair.

She owns her salon Karma Beauty Studio in Merrick New York for eighteen years and is married to her husband, Joey, since 1998.